THE IPFW
WRITING PROGRAM STUDENT HANDBOOK

Jennifer Stewart • Stevens Amidon

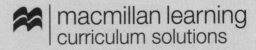

macmillan learning
curriculum solutions

bedford/st.martin's • hayden-mcneil • w.h. freeman • worth publishers

Printed in the United States of America

10 9 8 7 6 5 4 3 2 1

ISBN 978-0-7380-7966-0

Macmillan Learning Curriculum Solutions
14903 Pilot Drive
Plymouth, MI 48170
www.macmillanlearning.com

Huffman 7966-0 F16

INTRODUCTION

To the IPFW Writing Student:

The IPFW Writing Program Student Handbook was created for you to use in conjunction with the textbook for your writing classes. This handbook will help you understand the goals/outcomes of your writing course and the standards of performance expected of you. It also contains some writing program policies and procedures, links to IPFW resources, and some writing tips.

This handbook is required in all sections of ENG-W129, ENG-W131, and ENG-W233, and may be required in other writing courses. It may also be helpful as you write papers for other courses. For this reason, you should keep this book for use during your entire time at IPFW.

A handbook should not be read from page one through the end of the text, but instead its contents should be referenced as you need them. You should become familiar with the Table of Contents and use it to find information when you need it.

The appendices in the back of the handbook contain handouts to help you with your writing projects, as well as assignments and exercises for homework and class discussion. The pages are perforated so you can remove them and turn them in to your professor when asked.

We hope you enjoy your time at IPFW and we hope this handbook helps you become a better writer!

To the IPFW Instructor:

We hope you find the newest edition of the student handbook helpful. We have adopted a new reader-centered approach that focuses on questions you or the student might have about the Writing Program.

We want to make this the best handbook possible! If you find any errors, see any incorrect content, or have suggestions for new content, please let the Director of Writing know!

Jennifer Stewart

Stevens Amidon

Debrah Huffman, Director of Writing

ACKNOWLEDGMENTS

Many IPFW faculty and staff, both current and past, have had a hand in creating *The 2016–2017 IPFW Writing Program Student Handbook*. We would particularly like to acknowledge the following content contributors:

Tiff Adkins

Mary Schwartz

Stuart Blythe

Betsy Breitenbach

Cathleen Carosella

Karol Dehr

Debrah Huffman

Sara Webb-Sunderhaus

The IPFW Writing Center Staff

This handbook was also produced with the support and guidance of English Department faculty and staff, including:

Hardin Aasand

The English Department Composition Committee

The English Department Administrative Staff

Finally, I'd like to give a special thank you to Ryan Amidon, who did the copyediting for this edition. He also provided numerous suggestions to improve the usability of the handbook.

TABLE OF CONTENTS

1

WHY DO I NEED TO TAKE A WRITING COURSE?

Threshold Concept

"Succeeding in your writing course isn't just about producing a well-written paper. It's about learning a process that will help you be a successful writer in the university, as well as in the world beyond."

1.1 PURPOSE OF THE WRITING PROGRAM AT IPFW

Writing plays a major role in your ability to communicate both inside and outside the university. The Writing Program at IPFW is designed to make you a better student and a better communicator in the workplace and in all your personal interactions. Writing is not simply about producing texts but about learning throughout the writing process and gaining valuable critical thinking skills. Our writing courses will teach you how to better observe your world, its artifacts, and its texts. The courses will teach you how to interpret and analyze. They will teach you how to understand, evaluate, contend with, and organize ideas. And they will teach you how to conduct research—both firsthand research, and library research.

The skills you gain in these activities will go a long way towards making you a more successful student. They will also prepare you for the 21st century workplace. Corporate leaders tell us over and over again that the ability to skillfully engage in written and spoken communication is the most essential skill that they are looking for in potential employees. And we strongly believe that a democracy needs citizens able to engage with, and write about, public issues.

1.2 STRUCTURE OF THE WRITING PROGRAM AT IPFW

The Writing Program at IPFW offers a series of introductory and advanced courses to help you become a better writer and communicator. These are not the only writing courses offered at IPFW. The Department of English and Linguistics offers a variety of other courses in writing, literature, folklore, classics, and linguistics, for English majors and Writing minors, and to support professional programs, such as Nursing, Engineering, and Education. Regardless of your major, these courses play a central role in your General Education program at IPFW and will prepare you for academic success, whatever you choose as your major.

1.2.1 ENG-W103 Introductory Creative Writing   3 Credits

This course introduces students to a number of types of creative writing, including poetry and fiction. It fulfills General Education Category B.7 (Interdisciplinary Ways of Knowing).

1.2.2 ENG-W129 Introductory Elementary Composition   3 Credits

IPFW uses a self-placement system to allow students to identify how they want to begin their writing instruction. Students who feel they are better served by taking a two-semester sequence may elect to take ENG-W129 followed by ENG-W131. ENG-W129 is not a remedial course—it teaches many of the concepts and techniques emphasized in ENG-W131 but does so at a more deliberative pace for students who feel they need more practice in writing. It counts three credits towards graduation but does not fulfill any requirements of the General Education Program.

1.2.3 ENG-W131 Reading, Writing, and Inquiry I   3 Credits

This is the course most students take to fulfill the General Education Category A.1 (Written Communication) requirement. It focuses heavily on writing argumentative papers and analysis.

1.2.4 ENG-W140 Elementary Composition Honors   3 Credits

This course is limited to students admitted into IPFW's Honors Program. It combines the curriculum from ENG-W131 and ENG-W233 into a single, condensed, high-paced course. It fulfills both the General Education Category A.1 (Written Communication) requirement as well as the advanced writing requirement for most programs.

1.2.5 ENG-R190 Rhetorical Reading   3 Credits

While some students enter this course via placement testing, many students take this course as an elective because it prepares them for the kind of complex texts they will have to read and analyze while at college. This kind of complex analysis is one of the fundamental differences between the high school and college experiences. It can be taken alongside ENG-W131, ENG-W129, or as a stand-alone elective. It fulfills General Education Category B.7 (Interdisciplinary Ways of Knowing).

1.2.6 ENG-W203 Creative Writing   3 Credits

This course continues to introduce you to creative writing, but individual sections of this course focus on a specific genre, or type of writing, such as poetry or fiction. This course may be repeated for additional credit. It fulfills General Education Category B.7 (Interdisciplinary Ways of Knowing).

1.2.7 ENG-W232 Introduction to Business Writing   3 Credits

This course introduces students to many types of business writing and to business writing style. It is required by several majors and is good preparation if you work in a job that requires you to write. It fulfills General Education Category A.1 (Written Communication).

1.2.8 ENG-W233 Intermediate Expository Writing   3 Credits

This course introduces students to primary and secondary research, and research documentation and writing. It fulfills the advanced writing requirement for most programs in the College of Arts and Sciences and is required by many professional programs. It fulfills General Education Category A.1 (Written Communication).

1.2.9 ENG-W234 Technical Report Writing   3 Credits

This course introduces students to many types of writing used in science, engineering, and technology. It also introduces students to the use of graphics in written reports. It is required by several majors and is good preparation for workplace writing. It fulfills General Education Category A.1 (Written Communication).

1.2.10 ENG-W331 Business and Administrative Writing   3 Credits

This course focuses on business reports and introduces students to a number of kinds of business reports. It is required by a variety of majors in the College of Business and is good preparation for workplace writing in general.

1.2.11 ENG-W421 Technical Writing Projects   3 Credits

This course focuses on presenting and documenting technological information to both technical and non-technical audiences. It introduces students to presentations and technical research reports, and it teaches students to properly integrate graphics into these reports. It is required by several majors, and it fulfills General Education Category C.8 (Capstone).

1

1

1.3 USING WRITING COURSES TO MEET YOUR GENERAL EDUCATION CORE

With all of these courses, it can be confusing to figure out how they fit into the General Education program. The following table should help.

WRITING COURSE	COUNTS FOR GRADUATION CREDIT	FULFILLS THIS GENERAL EDUCATION COMPETENCY	CAN BE USED TO FULFILL GENERAL EDUCATION ELECTIVES*
ENG-W103	Yes	B.7 Interdisciplinary	Yes
ENG-W129	Yes	None	No
ENG-W131	Yes	A.1 Written Communication	Yes
ENG-W140	Yes	A.1 Written Communication	Yes
ENG-R190	Yes	B.7 Interdisciplinary	Yes
ENG-W203	Yes	B.7 Interdisciplinary	Yes
ENG-W232	Yes	A.1 Written Communication	Yes
ENG-W233	Yes	A.1 Written Communication	Yes
ENG-W234	Yes	A.1 Written Communication	Yes
ENG-W331	Yes	None	No
ENG-W421	Yes	C.8 Capstone	Yes

* If a writing course is not being used to fulfill one of the eight General Education Competency Areas, it can be used to fulfill 3 of the 9 elective credits in the General Education program.

Figure 1-1. Writing Courses and General Education Requirements.

These writing courses can help put you on a solid foundation for success in college and in the workplace. It is a good idea to talk to your advisor about the courses that best meet your own specific needs.

1.4 GETTING A MINOR IN WRITING

A minor in writing can be a great way to tell prospective employers that you have solid communication skills. This can be particularly true if you are majoring in a career field like engineering or nursing.

The Department of English and Linguistics offers writing minors in two areas: Professional Writing, which is focused on business and technical communication, and Creative Writing. Both minors require 15 credits of classwork in writing. If you are interested in adding such a minor, or are interested in learning which courses you would need to take for the minor, contact the department office by phone at 481-6841, or in person in LA 145, to make an appointment with a member of our faculty.

1

1

2

WHAT ARE MY RESPONSIBILITIES AS A STUDENT?

Threshold Concept

"If you take the time to get to know your instructors, and if you take the time to understand their expectations, you will succeed in college."

2.1 STUDENT RESPONSIBILITIES

In most classes instructors will have certain expectations of your commitment and dedication to your class. Listed below are some examples of responsibilities you should expect to take on in a writing course.

2.1.1 Commitments

Time: Instructors will expect that you dedicate anywhere from two to five hours of out-of-class work per week. This work could be composing essays, conducting research, or completing assignments. This amount of time required for out-of-class work is average; you may require more time to be successful in your writing class.

Initiative: Most instructors will expect you to be committed and dedicated to the class; however, your instructor won't know if you're confused or lost on an assignment or in the class. It's your responsibility to talk to your instructor for help if you need further guidance or explanation.

Respect: You are expected to show respect to your instructor, your fellow classmates, and yourself. In some classes, you may discuss sensitive or controversial material. Your instructor will expect you to address this material in a mature and reasoned fashion.

> **TIP: STAYING ON TOP OF YOUR WORK**
> Take advantage of the free IPFW Student Handbook Planner you receive. Many students become overwhelmed with the amount of homework and assignments they receive throughout the semester. Keeping all work written in one place helps prevent missed assignments.

2

Dedication: Instructors will expect you to keep up with the assignments in the daily portion of the class syllabus. You are expected to arrive to class prepared and on time.

2.1.2 Talking to Your Instructor

Check the syllabus and/or assignment sheets for any information that you should know already. Try not to ask an instructor "When are your office hours?" if those times are listed on the syllabus, Blackboard page, or assignment sheet. You will find Generic Assignment Templates in the back of Appendix A of this handbook. These templates will help you ask the "right questions" if your instructor is making an assignment orally.

If you are discussing a reading assignment, paper, test, or lecture in class, make sure that you've reviewed the material and are ready for the discussion. If you are unclear about points, okay, but that's no excuse for not reading the entire reading assignment or paper.

TIP: TALKING TO YOUR INSTRUCTOR

If you want to review a paper or have many questions to ask, consider emailing the paper or the questions to your instructor before the meeting. This might help him/her give you more thorough responses.

If you are absent, ask someone else in the class for notes (ask them before the day, if you know you're going to be absent) and NEVER, NEVER ask an instructor the following: "Did I miss anything?"

If you are struggling, explain what you are finding difficult, but don't complain about the class, the material, the lectures, etc. Search for how to improve, not just a quick fix. Sometimes your answer will have nothing to do with the material: improving your study skills, changing your study habits, setting up a study group, and using tutoring or supplemental instructions are all solid approaches that will help you succeed.

Most instructors are more than willing to discuss matters related to, but not necessarily covered in, the class—don't be afraid to talk about other areas of the topic or field that you find interesting or want to research.

Remember that instructors can be just as shy or awkward as any other person. So don't interpret formality as a dislike of students (or you). However, don't be surprised if your instructor is just as friendly as your next door neighbor.

2.2 INSTRUCTOR RESPONSIBILITIES

Just as you have responsibilities as a student, instructors have responsibilities to their class. Listed below are some of the responsibilities an instructor should maintain.

- **Availability:** Instructors should have clear office hours during which you can meet with them to discuss questions or concerns you may have about the course.

- **Time:** Class should not begin before or end after the scheduled time.
- **Clarity:** Instructors should clearly offer the following information:
  - Office location and hours
  - Textbook and supplies
  - Departmental goals for the course (see chapter 3 of this handbook)
  - Policies on (a) late work, (b) attendance and promptness, (c) plagiarism, (d) formatting of word-processed texts
  - Clear weighting of grades for major components of class
  - A detailed daily class schedule
- **Respect:** Instructors should foster a respectful learning environment in the classroom.

2.3 ACADEMIC HONESTY

You are expected to maintain academic honesty in all your courses. Plagiarizing, copying homework, and reusing a paper from a previous class can all be forms of academic dishonesty. The *IPFW Undergraduate Bulletin* describes plagiarism as "a form of cheating in which the work of someone else is offered as one's own. The language or ideas thus taken from another may range from isolated formulae, sentences, or paragraphs, to entire articles copied from printed sources, speeches, software, or the work of other students." To borrow someone else's writing without acknowledging that use is the worst form of academic dishonesty, which can result in failure for the course as well as sanction from the university. Similarly, "ghost writing" a paper can lead to sanctions from the university. Remember, you should **never** do someone else's homework for them.

You must do your own original work in your courses—and document that portion of your work that is collaborative with others, or borrowed from others, or that is your own work from other contexts. Whenever you quote passages, borrow graphics, or use ideas from others, you are legally and ethically obliged to acknowledge that use, following appropriate conventions for documenting sources.

FYI

FYI: PLAGIARISM

Often, beginning writing students fear they are plagiarizing. More advanced writing students occasionally cite improperly and, therefore, plagiarize. If you're unsure whether or not you're plagiarizing, your best bet is to take your draft to your instructor and **ask**. Fixing outright or unintentional plagiarism at the draft stage is the best way to avoid plagiarism penalties.

You may revise work that you have previously done or are doing in other courses for your writing course as long as it meets the following conditions: (1) it is your own work, (2) you plan an extensive revision for this course, and (3) you have informed, and have received the approval of, your instructor. If you have doubts about whether or not you are using your own or others' writing ethically and legally, ask your instructor.

2

2

Further information on plagiarism, including the forms the instructor uses to report such an offense, can be found on the website of the office of the IPFW Dean of Students.

2.3.1 Policy on Academic Honesty

Academic honesty is expected of all students. You are responsible for knowing how to maintain academic honesty and for abstaining from cheating, the appearance of cheating, and permitting or assisting in another's cheating.

Instructors are responsible for fostering the intellectual honesty as well as the intellectual development of students, and for applying methods of teaching, examination, and assignments that discourage student dishonesty. If necessary, instructors should explain clearly any specialized meanings of cheating and plagiarism as they apply to a specific course.

Your instructor will thoroughly investigate signs of academic dishonesty, take appropriate actions, and report such activity properly to prevent repeated offenses and to ensure equity.

2.3.2 Procedures

An instructor who has evidence of cheating will initiate a process to determine guilt or innocence and the penalty, if any, to be imposed, using the forms at the website of the office of the IPFW Dean of Students.

During an informal conference held within ten (10) class days of discovering the alleged cheating, your instructor will inform you of charges and evidence and allow you to present a defense. Your instructor will make an initial determination after this conference. You may be assigned a grade of Incomplete (I) if the matter cannot be fully resolved before course grades are due.

2.3.3 Reporting

During the period in which you are permitted to drop courses, the instructor will inform the registrar promptly of any allegation of cheating, so that you cannot withdraw from the course. The instructor who makes an initial finding that academic dishonesty has been practiced will propose an academic sanction. Then, within ten (10) class days, the instructor will supply a written report to you, the chair of your department, the dean or director of your school or division, and the dean of students. The report will summarize the evidence and penalties proposed.

2.3.4 Appeal

If your course grade is affected by the penalty, you have the right to appeal the penalty imposed by an instructor in accordance with the Grade Appeals policy.

2.4 GRADE APPEALS

As detailed in the *IPFW Undergraduate Bulletin*, if you wish to appeal your course grade, you must follow the policy as outlined in that bulletin.

The Grade Appeals Policy applies to all students enrolled at IPFW. It can be used by any student who has evidence or believes that evidence exists to show that a course grade was assigned, or a similar evaluation was made as a result of **prejudice, caprice, or other improper condition such as mechanical error**.

The English Department Grade Appeal Guidelines handout will help you determine if you have a legitimate basis for a grade appeal and will help guide you through the process. This handout can be found in Appendix A of this handbook.

In appealing, you must support, in writing, the allegation that an improper decision has been made and you must specify the remedy sought. You should seek the assistance of the Dean of Students in pursuing the appeal. During an appeal, the burden of proof is on you, except in the case of alleged academic dishonesty, where the instructor must support the allegation. You may have an advisor or friend present during all meetings with faculty members, administrators, and/or committees; he or she may advise you but may not speak on your behalf during the meetings.

TIP: GRADE APPEALS
If you are upset about a grade, WAIT before you go see your instructor. Put the test/paper aside and look at it again later.

Grades may be changed only by a university authority upon the decision of the Grade Appeals Subcommittee or by the instructor any time prior to the decision of the Grade Appeals Subcommittee.

2.4.1 Appeal Deadlines and Procedures

Appeals must be initiated no later than the time specified in the *IPFW Undergraduate Bulletin*. You must meet the deadlines and follow the procedures in the bulletin if you want your grade appeal to be heard.

2

2

3

WHERE CAN I GET HELP?

Threshold Concept

"Learning is a social process. One of the secret skills of the most successful students is that they have the courage to ask for help when they need it!"

3.1 THE IMPORTANCE OF ASKING FOR HELP

A university like IPFW is a much more complex institution than what you might be used to in high school. It has many more resources to help you succeed. However, unlike high school, you must take the initiative to get help. Students who regularly ask for help are much more likely to succeed than students who do not ask for help. This is sometimes a challenge—after all, we are taught to be self-reliant, and sometimes it feels like we have somehow failed if we need help. But the truth is all of us need help with something, and your tuition and fee money pays for these services, so you should use them!

3.2 GETTING HELP WITH YOUR CLASSWORK

3.2.1 Your Instructor

IPFW instructors are available to meet with students, and most hold regular office hours. Some instructors prefer to make appointments by email, while others prefer to make appointments face-to-face. Don't expect your instructor to be available immediately after class or without an appointment. Sometimes your instructor may have this kind of flexibility, but other times they may have other meetings and classes to attend to. It is important when you go to your instructor for help that you have clear questions to ask. Sometimes going to your meeting with notes can be a helpful approach.

3

3.2.2 Tutoring

The tutoring center offers you assistance if you have questions about assignments, need formulas or information clarified, or would like to talk to someone about your subject. You will acquire a better understanding of the content, appropriate study skills, and critical thinking skills. These skills will enable you to become a more independent, confident learner and critical thinker—skills that allow efficient and effective learning here at the university and in your future career. You can make an appointment for one-on-one tutoring online via TutorTrac at http://www.ipfw.edu/offices/casa/tutoring/tutortrac.html, or you can stop by KT G21 for a drop-in tutoring session.

Note: Due to renovations in the Library and Kettler Hall, the location of some of these services may change during the school year.

3.2.3 The IPFW Writing Center

The Writing Center, located in Kettler Hall for Fall 2016 and in Helmke Library Spring 2017, is open Monday–Friday, as well as on Sunday. It offers you free, one-on-one help, in writing papers for any class. You may come at any stage of the writing process—it's a great place to brainstorm ideas for a paper as well as a place that can help you develop a revision plan. Appointments are recommended and can be made at http://www.ipfw.edu/writing. You should bring your syllabus and assignment to your consultation.

 FYI: WRITING CENTER HANDOUTS
The Writing Center offers handouts on academic writing, sources and citation, and grammar and usage. Throughout this text, we rely on information from some of the most used handouts.

The Writing Center also offers online consulting, free handouts, and workshops on a variety of topics. If you have questions about the Writing Center's services, check the website at http://www.ipfw.edu/writing.

You should always come prepared with specific questions when you come to the Writing Center. Handout 2, the Writing Center Pre-Consultation Reflection, is included in Appendix A of this handbook. Filling it out will make for a more productive consultation!

3.2.4 The Helmke Library

The Helmke Library is an excellent resource for high-quality information and research assistance. The library has a substantial collection of academic journals and books, both in print and online. Writing students specifically should take advantage of the many databases, tools, and guides on the library's website, located at http://library.ipfw.edu. Helmke's research librarians can provide assistance on how to select the best databases and other resources for your assignment. They are available every day the library is open, including evenings and weekends.

3.2.5 Research Librarians

Sometimes it's difficult to find quality research for your assignment. Other times you find several articles that offer the same information. When this happens, you may want to throw your hands up in the air, give up, and switch assignment topics. Before doing so, consider meeting with a research librarian. Our librarians have special expertise to help you find the best, most appropriate information for your assignment. The library has a specialist for every subject area taught on campus. They can talk with you in-person or online.

To connect with a librarian, visit the library's website at http://library.ipfw.edu and select "Ask A Librarian" to chat online, send an email, or schedule an appointment. You can also call the library at 260-481-6805 or stop by one of the Service Desks to ask a question or meet with a librarian.

3.2.6 Topic Guides

For those times when you can't meet with a research librarian, Helmke librarians have designed Topic Guides for you in a variety of subject areas. These guides can help you find books, scholarly articles, primary sources, and more. Many of the Topic Guides are designed for specific courses. For example, there is a guide for ENG W129/W131 that provides the library resources most frequently needed by students taking these courses. To see a complete list of the library's Topic Guides, visit the Helmke Library website at http://library.ipfw.edu and select the Topic Guides button.

3.3 GETTING HELP WITH TECHNOLOGY

Technology Support Services (http://www.ipfw.edu/offices/osa/technology-support-services-for-ipfw-students.html) is the first place you should go for support.

3.3.1 Other Technological Assistance

Sometimes you need support quickly, or you have a problem that you haven't been able to successfully solve. The Information Technology Service (ITS), located in KT 206, offers you technological assistance and facilities on campus. If you need help configuring your iPad to the university wireless network or activating your email account, ITS is a great place to go.

3

3

The ITS Help Desk has a variety of tools and technicians to help you troubleshoot computer or software problems. For assistance, stop by KT 206 or call the Help Desk at 260-481-6030.

3.3.2 Facilities and Services

Computer labs are located in Kettler Hall, Neff Hall, Helmke Library, Science Building, and Walb Union. Student computer labs are staffed with lab consultants. Generally, the lab consultants can answer various technical questions you may have; however, consultants will not teach a specific program application (e.g., Microsoft Word). ITS also has established several software license agreements for home use of many software programs. These software programs are offered at a greatly reduced price for students. Most purchases can be made at Follett's Bookstore with proof of enrollment—generally a current schedule of classes is required.

3.4 ADDITIONAL GENERAL HELP

3.4.1 Getting Help with Your Schedule, or with Graduation Requirements

Your academic advisor is the expert on these issues. If you don't know who your advisor is, log in to "My IPFW" and find the name of your advisor. If you have declared a major, contact your academic department to have an advisor assigned to you. If you haven't yet declared your major, contact the Mastodon Advising Center in KT 109, phone number 260-481-6595.

3.4.2 Getting Help with Money

More students leave college for financial reasons than any other cause. In many cases, such withdrawals can be prevented. If you are having difficulty making payments to IPFW, contact the Bursar's Office in KT G57. If your financial circumstances have changed or if you need more financial assistance, make an appointment to talk to a counselor in the Financial Aid Office, KT 103, phone number 260-481-6820. The counselor can often provide you with help or explain to you the process for appealing a financial aid decision.

3.4.3 Getting Help with Personal Problems

The IPFW Student Assistance Program (SAP) offers help with everything from family problems to helping you overcome a substance abuse problem. SAP is located in Walb 113, and is jointly administered by IPFW and Parkview Hospital. Its phone number is

260-266-8060/800-721-8809. The SAP is committed to offering you a place to discuss these kinds of matters in a safe environment where the privacy of your personal health information is maintained.

3

3

4

WHAT ARE THE GOALS
OF MY COURSE?

Threshold Concept
"Writers are made not born. By working through these outcomes, you can become a confident and competent writer."

4.1 COURSE OUTCOMES FOR ENG-W131, ENG-W232, ENG-W233, AND ENG-W234

These course outcomes were developed as part of the Indiana General Education Common Core Initiative. These outcomes should ensure you have the writing skills necessary for college and beyond. While these courses share the same outcomes, the specific approach to achieving these outcomes and the level of proficiency expected in meeting these outcomes differ. For example, while ENG-W131 focuses on argument, critical reading, and analysis, ENG-W233 builds on these skills by asking students to argue, read, and analyze through the lens of primary and secondary academic research. ENG-W232 does the same through the lens of business writing and research, while ENG-W234 does the same through the lens of technical writing and research.

A.1 Written Communication Competency
Upon completion of this course, students will be able to:

1.1. Produce texts that use appropriate formats, genre conventions, and documentation styles while controlling tone, syntax, grammar, and spelling.
1.2. Demonstrate an understanding of writing as a social process that includes multiple drafts, collaboration, and reflection.
1.3. Read critically, summarize, apply, analyze, and synthesize information and concepts in written and visual texts as the basis for developing original ideas and claims.
1.4. Demonstrate an understanding of writing assignments as a series of tasks including identifying and evaluating useful and reliable outside sources.

4

1.5. Develop, assert and support a focused thesis with appropriate reasoning and adequate evidence.

1.6. Compose texts that exhibit appropriate rhetorical choices, which include attention to audience, purpose, context, genre, and convention.

1.7. Demonstrate proficiency in reading, evaluating, analyzing, and using material collected from electronic sources (such as visual, electronic, library databases, Internet sources, other official databases, federal government databases, reputable blogs, wikis, etc.).

1.8. Demonstrate proficiency in reading, evaluating, analyzing, and using material collected from electronic sources (such as visual, electronic, library databases, Internet sources, other official databases, federal government databases, reputable blogs, wikis, etc.).

FYI: W131/W233 DIFFERENCES

ENG-W233 assumes you have built a foundation for writing in your ENG-W131 course. While the W131 course focuses on persuasive writing and analytical writing, W233 focuses on developing your writing skills by engaging in research, and by analyzing your rhetorical choices and your research methods.

4.2 COURSE OUTCOMES FOR ENG-W129

The course outcomes for ENG-W129 were developed to prepare you for success in ENG-W131 and other courses you will take at IPFW.

1. **Rhetorical Knowledge**: Upon completion of the course, students should be able to focus on a purpose; define a thesis; respond to the needs of different audiences; adopt an appropriate stance toward audience and topic; and write in several genres.

2. **Critical Thinking, Reading, and Writing**: Upon completion of the course students should be able to use writing and reading for inquiry, learning, and thinking; be able to paraphrase and summarize the work of others; and integrate their own ideas with those of others.

3. **Processes**: Upon completion of the courses, students should use multiple drafts to complete an effective text; develop flexible strategies for generating, revising, and editing; engage in a recursive process of writing; demonstrate that they understand the collaborative and social aspects of writing processes; learn to critique their own and others' work; and use various technologies to address a range of audiences.

4. **Knowledge of Conventions**: Upon completion of the courses, students should demonstrate that they can recognize and use common formats for different genres of texts; practice appropriate means of documenting their work; and control syntax, grammar, punctuation, and spelling.

FYI: W129/W131 DIFFERENCES

While the outcomes for these writing courses may look similar, the kinds of assignments, methods, and requirements an instructor may use to meet these outcomes will vary significantly.

4.3 COURSE OUTCOMES FOR ENG-W103

These course outcomes were developed as part of the Indiana General Education Common Core Initiative. These outcomes are designed to help you use the process of producing a creative performance to better understand nature and the human experience.

B.7 Interdisciplinary or Creative Ways of Knowing Competency
Upon completion of this course, students will be able to:

1.1. Produce texts that use appropriate formats, genre conventions, and documentation styles while controlling tone, syntax, grammar, and spelling.

1.2. Demonstrate an understanding of writing as a social process that includes multiple drafts, collaboration, and reflection.

1.6. Compose texts that exhibit appropriate rhetorical choices, which include attention to audience, purpose, context, genre, and convention.

7.1. Demonstrate an understanding of the creative process using the vocabulary of the appropriate discipline.

7.2. Perform or create a work of personal expression and bring the work to fruition using applicable skills.

7.3. Articulate a reflective and critical evaluation of their own and others' creative efforts using written and/or oral communication.

4.4 COURSE OUTCOMES FOR ENG-W203

These course outcomes were developed as part of the Indiana General Education Common Core Initiative. These outcomes are designed to help you use the process of producing a creative performance to better understand nature and the human experience. While W103 and W203 are both creative writing courses, each section of W203 focuses on a single genre of writing, either fiction or poetry.

B.7 Interdisciplinary or Creative Ways of Knowing Competency
Upon completion of this course, students will be able to:

1.6. Compose texts that exhibit appropriate rhetorical choices, which include attention to audience, purpose, context, genre, and convention.

6.1 Recognize and describe humanistic, historical, or artistic works or problems and patterns of the human experience.

4

6.2   Apply disciplinary methodologies, epistemologies, and traditions of the humanities and the arts, including the ability to distinguish primary and secondary sources.

6.3   Analyze and evaluate texts, objects, events, or ideas in their cultural, intellectual, or historical contexts.

6.4   Analyze the concepts and principles of various types of humanistic or artistic expression.

6.5   Create, interpret, or reinterpret artistic and/or humanistic works through performance or criticism.

6.6   Develop arguments about forms of human agency or expression grounded in rational analysis and in an understanding of and respect for spatial, temporal, and cultural contexts.

6.7   Analyze diverse narratives and evidence in order to explore the complexity of human experience across space and time.

7.1   Demonstrate an understanding of the creative process using the vocabulary of the appropriate discipline.

7.2   Perform or create a work of personal expression and bring the work to fruition using applicable skills.

7.3   Articulate a reflective and critical evaluation of their own and others' creative efforts using written and/or oral communication.

4.5 COURSE OUTCOMES FOR ENG-R190

These course outcomes were developed as part of the Indiana General Education Common Core Initiative. These outcomes are designed to help you approach the reading of texts in a broadly interdisciplinary way. It does so by teaching you the principles of rhetorical reading.

Upon completion of this course, students will be able to:

1.3.   Read critically, summarize, apply, analyze, and synthesize information and concepts in written and visual texts as the basis for developing original ideas and claims.

1.5.   Develop, assert and support a focused thesis with appropriate reasoning and adequate evidence.

1.7.   Demonstrate proficiency in reading, evaluating, analyzing, and using material collected from electronic sources (such as visual, electronic, library databases, Internet sources, other official databases, federal government databases, reputable blogs, wikis, etc.).

5.2 Identify the strengths and weaknesses of contending explanations or interpretations for social, behavioral, or historical phenomena.

5.4 Evaluate evidence supporting conclusions about the behavior of individuals, groups, institutions, or organizations.

6.2 Apply disciplinary methodologies, epistemologies, and traditions of the humanities and the arts, including the ability to distinguish primary and secondary sources.

6.3 Analyze and evaluate texts, objects, events, or ideas in their cultural, intellectual, or historical contexts.

6.4 Analyze the concepts and principles of various types of humanistic or artistic expression.

6.6 Develop arguments about forms of human agency or expression grounded in rational analysis and in an understanding of and respect for spatial, temporal, and cultural contexts.

4.6 COURSE OUTCOMES FOR ENG-W331

1. **Rhetorical Knowledge**: Upon completion of the course, students should be able to focus on a purpose; define a thesis; respond to the needs of business and organizational audiences; adopt an appropriate stance toward audience and topic; and write in several report genres.

2. **Critical Thinking, Reading, and Writing**: Upon completion of the course students should be able to use writing and reading for inquiry, learning, and thinking; be able to paraphrase and summarize the work of others; and integrate their own ideas with those of others.

3. **Processes**: Upon completion of the course, students should use multiple drafts to complete an effective text; develop flexible strategies for generating, revising, and editing; engage in a recursive process of writing; demonstrate that they understand the collaborative and social aspects of writing processes; learn to critique their own and others' work; and use various technologies to address a range of audiences.

4. **Knowledge of Conventions**: Upon completion of the course, students should demonstrate that they can recognize and use common formats for different genres of texts; practice appropriate means of documenting their work; and control syntax, grammar, punctuation, and spelling.

5. **Working in Multiple Media**: Upon completion of the course, students should demonstrate the ability to produce texts for print, electronic media, and oral delivery.

4

4.7 COURSE OUTCOMES FOR ENG-W421

These course outcomes were developed as part of the Indiana General Education Common Core Initiative. These outcomes are designed to help you have a capstone experience at IPFW.

C.8 Capstone
Upon completion of the capstone, students will be able to:

8.1. Produce an original work involving the creation or application of knowledge, performance, or service.

8.2. Report the results of original work through a discipline-appropriate product.

8.3. Demonstrate a high level of personal integrity and professional ethics by understanding the ethical responsibilities related to the profession associated with the subject of the capstone project.

8.4. Demonstrate critical-thinking abilities and familiarity with quantitative and/or qualitative reasoning.

4.8 THE IPFW BACCALAUREATE FRAMEWORK

While the outcomes for the writing courses are very specific, they are only one part of your university education. IPFW faculty have established a framework on which all IPFW students' educations are built. Listed below are the six foundations to a baccalaureate education at IPFW:

- **Acquisition of Knowledge**: Students will demonstrate breadth of knowledge across disciplines and depth of knowledge in their chosen discipline. In order to do so, students must demonstrate the requisite information-seeking skills and technological competencies.
- **Application of Knowledge**: Students will demonstrate the ability to integrate and apply that knowledge and, in so doing, demonstrate the skills necessary for life-long learning.
- **Personal and Professional Values**: Students will demonstrate the highest levels of personal integrity and professional ethics.
- **A Sense of Community**: Students will demonstrate the knowledge and skills necessary to be productive and responsible citizens and leaders in local, regional, national, and international communities. In so doing, students will demonstrate a commitment to free and open inquiry and mutual respect across multiple cultures and perspectives.
- **Critical Thinking and Problem Solving**: Students will demonstrate facility and adaptability in their approach to problem solving. In so doing, students will demonstrate critical-thinking abilities and familiarity with quantitative and qualitative reasoning.

- **Communication**: Students will demonstrate the written, oral, and multimedia skills necessary to communicate effectively in diverse settings.

ASSIGNMENT LINK 1
For a better understanding of how your writing course connects with the IPFW Baccalaureate Framework, go to Assignment 1 in Appendix B of this handbook.

4

5

WHAT IS RHETORIC, AND WHY SHOULD I LEARN ABOUT IT?

Threshold Concept

"The single most effective step you can take to improve your writing is to ask: 'What is the purpose of this text?' and 'Who is the audience for this text?'"

5.1 THE BIRTH OF RHETORIC

Both writing and public speaking are based upon theories of rhetoric. Rhetoric has a long tradition as a field of study in American universities. In fact, John Quincy Adams served as Boylston Professor of Rhetoric and Oratory after completing his term as the sixth president of the United States.

Rhetoric emerged as a significant field with the birth of the Greek democracy. Democracy creates legislatures and courts where citizens must plead their cases. The ability to effectively present an argument and persuade members of a group becomes greatly valued in a democracy.

Traditional histories tell us that the first rhetorician was Corax of Sicily in the 5th century B.C. About a hundred years later, Gorgias of Leontini, Sicilian ambassador to Athens, brought rhetoric to the Greeks.

5.2 DEFINING RHETORIC

Rhetoric can be defined in many ways. Our culture has often used the term in a negative way, for example, referring to a political speech as "empty rhetoric." A common definition for rhetoric used today is "an exaggerated or unsupported argument, or use of language."

Historically, rhetoric has been defined much more positively. The Greek philosopher Aristotle defined rhetoric as "the art of discovering the means of persuasion for any subject."

5

A more modern definition sees rhetoric as a form of negotiation between a reader and a writer, via a text.

JOURNAL PROMPT 1

What differences do you see in these three definitions? When have you used rhetoric in your own life?

5.3 RHETORICAL APPEALS

Aristotle believed there were three methods of persuading an audience:

1. Logos: using logic
2. Pathos: using emotion
3. Ethos: using credibility

While we can separate these appeals to study them, most effective writers use all three appeals to move their audiences.

ASSIGNMENT LINK 2

Want to learn more about the appeals? Go to Assignment 2 in Appendix B of this handbook.

5.4 THE RHETORICAL TRIANGLE

One way of better understanding how rhetoric functions is through the following visual (Figure 5-1) derived from Aristotle, commonly called the rhetorical triangle.

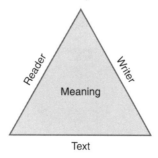

Figure 5-1. The Rhetorical Triangle.

The reader, the writer, and the text all work together to make meaning. Adding an additional element brings Aristotle's formula closer to a modern definition.

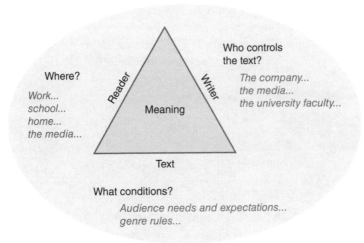

Figure 5-2. Context.

Context is the *where* of the text, as in where, or under what conditions, is the work written.

- **4 Categories of Context** (from Lauer, *Four Worlds of Writing*)
  1. Everyday life
  2. School
  3. Work
  4. Public sphere
- **4 Aims of Writing** (from Kinneavy, *Aims of Discourse*)
  James Kinneavy, a rhetorician and priest, looked at the rhetorical triangle and realized that each element of rhetoric could be associated with a type of writing or speaking (discourse).

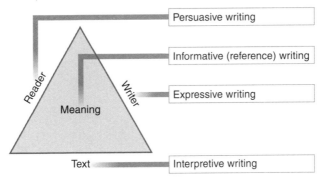

Figure 5-3. Kinneavy's Aims of Discourse.

5

Persuasive writing focuses on the reader who you want to persuade. In *Expressive Writing* you are mostly interested in simply getting your thoughts on paper, with little regard to audience. In *Interpretive Writing* you are primarily focused on analyzing or making sense of a text. And in *Informative Writing* you aim to get information to the reader as clearly and concisely as possible. Of course, most pieces of writing contain more than one of these elements, though usually one of them is dominant.

5.4.1 Writing Genres

When you write with a specific *aim*, in a specific *context*, you will often find yourself following the rules of a specific kind of writing. The Greek word for "kind" or "type" is *genre*, and we use that term to refer to forms of writing that recur over and over again. For example, if you have a job selling cars, you might write a persuasive text in your work context that we call a "sales pitch." If you have to write a paper for school interpreting the characters in *Hamlet*, you will probably follow the rules or conventions for writing a "literary analysis." If you want to get something off your chest, you might express yourself privately in a journal or publicly in a blog.

As you write, you should ask yourself these questions:

- Why am I writing?
- What context am I writing for?
- Who am I writing for?
- Why do they care?
- What do I want them to do/think/believe?
- Is there a writing genre that fits my purpose and context? What are some rules for using this genre?

ASSIGNMENT LINK 3

Want to learn more about genres? Go to Assignment 3 in Appendix B of this handbook.

6

WHAT DOES ALL THIS TALK ABOUT CRITICAL THINKING MEAN?

Threshold Concept

"Spending some quality time with the invention process, by thinking critically about what you read and observe in the world, will do far more to improve your writing than focusing on grammar, punctuation, or other editing concerns."

6.1 CRITICAL THINKING AND THE BACCALAUREATE FRAMEWORK

We've all heard the term critical thinking. In fact the term is used so often that we rarely think about what it means—we just take it for granted. That's unfortunate, because critical thinking encompasses the central set of skills that makes your college education valuable. That is why critical thinking plays such a central role in the IPFW Baccalaureate Framework. So let's begin our discussion of critical thinking by reviewing that section of the framework again.

Critical Thinking and Problem Solving: *Students will demonstrate facility and adaptability in their approach to problem solving. In so doing, students will demonstrate critical-thinking abilities and familiarity with quantitative and qualitative reasoning.*

—from the IPFW Baccalaureate Framework

We will read this closely by looking at some important terms. We notice right away that critical thinking is linked with problem solving. Why? Because before you can solve a problem you must understand it. Two other terms are used here that you may not understand—qualitative and quantitative reasoning. The best way to understand these terms is to examine two situations where researchers are trying to solve problems.

Mary is a Biology major who is conducting an experiment in her biology lab. She has grown 100 samples of a common bacteria in Petri dishes. She treats 50 of the samples with one kind of antibiotic and 50 of the samples with a different antibiotic. The purpose of the experiment is to determine which antibiotic works best at inhibiting the growth of the bacterium. After treatment, she periodically weighs each sample and records that weight to measure the bacterial growth. She will use statistics to analyze these measurements and determine the differences in performance of the antibiotics. This use of numbers and statistics to analyze information is what we call *quantitative reasoning*.

John has a work-study job serving as Assistant Director of the university writing center. He notices that most of the engineering students seem to be signing up for appointments with one specific tutor who has a very busy schedule, while other tutors are being underutilized. He decides to research this problem by interviewing a sample of the tutors and the engineering students. The purpose of this study is to determine if the writing center can better serve the needs of these engineering students. He designs a series of interview questions, conducts the interviews, and analyzes the verbal data he collected by looking for areas where answers can be grouped together by theme or topic. He discovers that most writing tutors are English majors, and that many of these majors feel unprepared when asked to help with engineering writing. He also learns that the engineering students are signing up for the one specific tutor because one of the engineering students made a Facebook entry about how helpful the tutor was with her engineering writing. He also discovers that the tutor mentioned feels very comfortable with engineering writing because she completed a technical writing internship as part of her English major. Based on this data, John designs a program to better prepare the writing center tutors to work with engineering students. This analysis of verbal data gathered from interviews or visual data gathered from field observations are examples of what we call *qualitative reasoning*.

The use of analysis and synthesis is a central feature of critical thinking. When we *analyze* information, we are attacking a problem by breaking it down into parts and examining those parts to better understand the problem. When we *synthesize* information, we take what we have learned from analysis, and put the parts together in a new way to solve the problem.

There are many ways in which you will be asked to analyze and synthesize information in your writing classes and throughout your college career. Your writing classes will help you become more adept at critical thinking by asking you to analyze information in increasingly sophisticated ways.

JOURNAL PROMPT 2

When have you used analysis and synthesis in your own life?

If you are taking W129, you may be asked to read a common nonfiction text and conduct a *Content Analysis* of that text. In W131, you will be expected to learn how to persuade or reason convincingly, and you will learn how to use *Rhetorical Analysis* to better understand how the writers of sophisticated nonfiction texts make language choices to better persuade their readers. In W233, you may be asked to conduct a *Genre Analysis* to better understand the ways in which scholarly articles are conducted. You may also be asked to conduct quantitative or qualitative research in W233.

6.2 ANALYZING CONTENT

Content Analysis focuses on the meaning of a text. Just like John had to read the interview data from his writing center research project very closely, looking for common or repetitive answers and important themes, the writer of a content analysis reads a text closely, looking for clues that better explain its meaning. The following questions may help you when you are analyzing content:

- **Are there words you don't understand?** Begin by looking up words you are uncertain about in a good dictionary.
- **What is the theme of the text?** The theme is the central idea or point that is being made and is often found explicitly stated in the introduction and/or conclusion of a nonfiction text. In fiction, the theme is rarely stated so explicitly, but instead the central idea surfaces through a character's thoughts, the main action of the narrative, or literary devices such as repeated use of a metaphor or allegory.
- **What problem is the text trying to solve?** Some texts explore problems and propose solutions. Often they do so by comparing and contrasting various approaches to an issue and use evidence to explain why one approach is superior. A close reader should attend to the kind and quality of the evidence the writer uses.
- **How should the text be read?** In many nonfiction texts, you can answer this question by simply summarizing the material. In a short text you can do this line by line—we call such line by line analysis an *explication*. In literary texts, there are often a number of ways a text can be read, and you might, for example,

> **ASSIGNMENT LINK 4**
> For an example of a Content Analysis assignment often used by ENG-W129 instructors, go to Assignment 4 in Appendix B of this handbook.

write an analysis comparing and contrasting the various ways in which critics have read a text. Or you might choose a specific lens, such as *feminism* or *religion* or a literary theory such as *deconstruction*, and persuade your reader why that is a useful way to interpret the text.

- **How is the work organized?** Does it have a beginning, a middle, and an end? Does it use a problem/solution organization? Does it depend on comparisons to make its meaning? Is it a narrative, does it tell a story? If so, how do the setting of the story, the characters, the plot, and the language work together to make meaning?
- **What assumptions does the writer make?** Are the assumptions warranted or unwarranted? Are there contradictions in the text?

6

6

6.3 ANALYZING RHETORIC

Where Content Analysis focuses on the meaning of the text, Rhetorical Analysis is concerned with discovering *how* the text makes meaning. In terms of the rhetorical triangle discussed in Chapter 5, Rhetorical Analysis uncovers the ways in which the reader, the writer, and the text all work together to make meaning. Aristotle's rhetorical appeals provide us with one good framework for exploring these relationships (your instructor may suggest others).

6.3.1 Logos

One of the strongest ways to reach an audience is an appeal to reason. These are some of the questions you should ask when exploring the ways in which a writer uses reasoning in a text to appeal to the readers:

- What claims does the writer make in the text?
- What kind of evidence does the writer use to support her claims?
- Are there fallacies in the reasoning?
- Does the writer anticipate objections to the claim, and does the writer address those objections in a fair and reasonable manner?
- Does the style used by the writer strengthen or weaken the power of the claims made? How and where?

6.3.2 Pathos

While the use of emotion in persuasion is sometimes seen as unprofessional or even unethical in some contexts, it remains

JOURNAL PROMPT 3

Examine a print or video advertisement. How does the advertisement use logos, pathos, and ethos to persuade you to purchase the product or service being advertised?

a powerful way to reach an audience. These questions should help you discover how the writer uses pathos to appeal to the readers:

- Who is the audience for this text? What are some of the values or beliefs this audience holds? How does the writer of the text use the audience's connection to its values to appeal to the reader?
- Does the writer use a formal or informal style when it comes to use of language and organization? How do these choices strengthen or weaken the emotional appeal of the text?
- Does the writer use his or her own experience to create empathy in the mind of the audience? How and where?
- Identify times when the writer shows or uses anger, shame, or passion in the text? How do these work to strengthen or weaken the argument?
- Does the writer work to create desire for an object, a service, or a value in the text? Does this desire strengthen or weaken the argument?

6.3.3 Ethos

Even the cleverest reasoning or the most powerful use of emotion will fail to persuade a reader if the writer cannot establish a level of trust or credibility with the audience. These questions can help you discover ways in which writers build such ethos:

- Does the writer's voice seem to be impartial, or at least fair and balanced? Why, or why not?
- Does the writer display a strong grasp of the subject matter being discussed? Does the writer use sources that appear credible, fair, and balanced?
- Does the writer use a style (formal or informal) that strengthens her credibility on the subject?
- Does the writer seem more concerned with others, and society as a whole, or with herself?
- Does the writer present her credentials to make this case in a direct or indirect manner?

ASSIGNMENT LINK 5

For an example of a Rhetorical Analysis assignment often used by ENG-W131 instructors, go to Assignment 5 in Appendix B of this handbook.

6.4 ANALYZING GENRE

Another form of Rhetorical Analysis focuses on the genre the writer has chosen to use. Remember from Chapter 5 that genres are specific kinds or types of writing with a set of rules. Often these rules are established formally or informally by a community of writers. You should ask these kinds of questions when conducting a Genre Analysis::

- What forum or journal published this text? Look up its website. Does it have a set of rules for publication?
- Is there a sponsoring organization for the journal or forum that published this text?
- Who is the intended audience for this genre? What type of things does the audience already know? Is there a kind of technical jargon used by this audience? If so, describe it.
- What kind of rules does this genre seem to expect the writer to follow?
- What kind of evidence is acceptable/expected in this genre? What level of formality is expected in this genre?

ASSIGNMENT LINK 6

For an example of a Genre Analysis assignment often used by ENG-W233 instructors, go to Assignment 6 in Appendix B of this handbook.

6

6

7

WHAT SHOULD I KNOW ABOUT RESEARCH AND WRITING?

Threshold Concept

"Whether you are a college student looking for information to write a paper, a homeowner who needs to figure out the best way to choose a roofing contractor, or a small business owner who needs to decide whether or not to develop a social media presence, you need the ability to find, evaluate, and use information. In an increasingly information-rich world, the ability to use information effectively is critical."

7.1 YOUR WRITING COURSE AND RESEARCH

No matter what writing course you are taking, you can expect that class to include some focus on research. In ENG-W131, you will be expected to write an argument or position paper supported with evidence you gather through research. In ENG-W233, you will be expected to complete an extended research paper, following academic research conventions. In business and technical writing courses you will be engaging in research practices adapted specifically to those fields. And while research practices vary greatly from discipline to discipline—the way a physicist does research is very different from the way in which a historian does research—there are some general principles you can follow that will make your research tasks easier.

7.2 CHOOSING YOUR RESEARCH TOPIC OR PROBLEM

The first step of a search strategy is to choose a problem to investigate. In other words, you need to define and describe the kind of information you need. In some cases you may have been assigned a list of topics from which to choose. If you are responsible for selecting your own research topic, here are some general suggestions:

- Find a topic that interests you and that you can make interesting to your reader.
- Limit yourself to an aspect of the topic that you can adequately research and write in the time allotted. Avoid broad generalities or narrow specialties.

- If you are doing secondary research, choose a topic that can be researched in IPFW's Helmke Library. You must be able to find the information that will support your ideas. By and large, the library does not collect materials that are not directly related to the curriculum.

7.2.1 Primary Research

Primary research is research you conduct yourself. In other words, you might gather information by conducting interviews, by observing an activity, through a survey, or by conducting an experiment. This kind of research can be particularly useful when you are conducting research to solve a local problem, such as a shortage of menu options delivered by campus food providers. Primary research can help you build credibility (ethos) by demonstrating your ability to identify a limited research question and a plan to gather information to answer that research question.

7.2.2 Secondary Research

Secondary research consists of gathering information from books, articles, newspapers, and websites in order to understand what others have discovered about a topic. In some cases, the purpose of secondary research will be to identify studies where other people have conducted primary research and reported their results. In other cases, an expert might be writing an opinion piece where she uses her expertise to analyze or evaluate an issue.

One of the best places to get started is an encyclopedia, handbook, or textbook. These tools will provide an overview of your topic and give you hints on ways to limit it. While you are using the encyclopedia, look for an outline at the beginning of the article or the boldface print and captions within the article. Be sure to note any special terminology, people's names, or events that might be useful in searching for information in other sources.

7.2.3 Connecting Your Topic or Problem to Research

Whether you are doing primary research or secondary research, or both, it is important that you connect your research with a larger conversation related to your subject. What does this mean? Consider the example given earlier, of a group of students conducting research investigating a shortage of menu options on campus. They may conduct primary research by (1) observing and cataloguing all the menu choices available on campus; and (2) surveying or interviewing students to discover the level of student interest in a broader choice of menu items. However, the students probably could make a better case for a proposal to broaden the menu choices by connecting the research to broader conversations about nutrition and obesity.

7.2.4 Developing Your Topic or Problem

You should begin your research with some background reading. A good encyclopedia, or even Wikipedia, can give you some background information on your subject. Searching for websites on a topic using a search engine like Google is another good way to develop this initial familiarity with your topic. After you have done some background reading, you should have some thoughts about how the topic can be developed. You may want to:

- Examine a problem or conflict
- Compare and contrast two ideas or individuals
- Consider the causes, effects, trends, or influences on your topic
- Describe a situation, person, corporation, or event
- Persuade your reader

While you determine how to develop your topic, you should also be considering whether your topic is too narrow or too broad to handle. Most people need to restrict their topic to more manageable proportions. Topics can be limited in several ways:

- Time: Concentrate on the 1970s (instead of the 20th century)
- Place: Focus on Iran (instead of the Middle East)
- Discipline: Take an anthropological, psychological, or economic view of your subject
- Specific Event: Examine Woodstock (instead of rock concerts)
- Specific Person (or Group or Work): Focus on Eleanor Roosevelt (instead of First Ladies)

Keep in mind that you can also limit your topic too much, setting unrealistic, "needle-in-the-haystack" search constraints.

7.2.5 Developing a Research Question

One of the best ways to develop a research paper is to identify a very specific question you want to answer. For example, for her ENG-W131 class, Mary was asked to write a paper where she takes a position on a controversial issue of some importance to her. She began by freewriting and discovered that what she most wanted to write about was the issue of body image among young women and the influence of media on promoting unhealthy body weights among teenage girls. She was particularly interested in demonstrating how fashion shows like *Project Runway* and *America's Next Top Model* idealize the female body in what she considered dangerous ways. When she began asking questions about her topic, she discovered that it seemed to revolve around four issues: (1) the ethics of idealizing certain kinds of body images on television; (2) the dangers of anorexia; (3) how audience and demographics affect the content of television programming; and (4) definitions of beauty and how those definitions affect the construction of gender identity. Mary decides that the first group of issues interested her most, and she decided she wanted to answer the question, "Should television networks be pressured to represent the female body in a more ethically responsible way?"

7.2.6 Finding Information

When you're asked to do research, you're most likely to head to the Internet. Perhaps you'll do a Google search. Maybe you'll use your browser's search engine. While this research

7

7

method is effective in determining who that one actor is or how to change the oil in your lawnmower, this method may not be the most effective place to begin your search for academic sources. Whether you have to use substantial and/or scholarly sources, Helmke Library is the best place to begin your source search.

7.3 USING SOURCES

7.3.1 Preliminary, Primary, and Secondary Sources

- **Preliminary Sources**—these are your pre-research sources. As you delve into a topic, you will most likely do a preliminary search through various databases, Internet sites, and IUCAT to ensure that your research topic is viable. As your research topic develops, you may not necessarily *use* all your preliminary sources, as they may no longer support your point.
- **Primary Sources**—this is the research *you conduct*. If you conduct an interview or survey, detail personal experience, perform an observation, execute an experiment, etc., it is your work, and thus, a primary source.
- **Secondary Sources**—this is the research *others have conducted*. When you cite from a book, article, film, study, etc., that is someone else's work, this is considered a secondary source. You have most likely used secondary sources more frequently than primary sources.

7.3.2 Popular, Trade/Professional, and Scholarly Sources

As you progress through your writing courses, your instructors will ask you to use more scholarly sources. The differences between popular, trade/professional, and scholarly are sometimes difficult to determine. Following are six areas to examine when determining what type of source you may have.

Article Content

What the author has to say and how the author makes his/her point can help you identify the type of source you've found.

POPULAR	TRADE/PROFESSIONAL	SCHOLARLY
Entertaining and/or informative material of interest to the general public; articles and paragraphs fairly short in length; common language used; assumes no previous knowledge of topic; no bibliography.	Articles are short; tend to not have abstracts; may or may not cite sources; tend to contain reports of research or news in the field rather than original studies; use language familiar to people in the profession.	Often contain original research on a narrowly focused topic; sometimes preceded by an abstract (summary) of the article; often use specialized terminology; assume some previous knowledge of the subject by the reader; sources are cited.
Information derived from "Is Your Journal Scholarly?", Helmke Library		

Figure 7-1. Article Content.

Purpose

Popular, trade/professional, and scholarly sources on a specific topic may have a similar general purpose; however, a close examination into the specific purpose of the article will reveal its true type.

POPULAR	TRADE/PROFESSIONAL	SCHOLARLY
To inform or entertain the general public; produced for profit; sold at newsstands.	To communicate trends, developments, product information, concepts, and applications useful to those working in a profession or industry.	To add to the body of knowledge in a discipline, often by reporting original research or recent experimentation; usually not-for-profit; distributed by subscription only to individuals or institutions like your university library.
Information derived from "Is Your Journal Scholarly?", Helmke Library		

Figure 7-2. Article Purpose.

7

Audience

The audience's knowledge of the topic varies based on the type of source you've selected.

POPULAR	TRADE/PROFESSIONAL	SCHOLARLY
Nonprofessionals, laypeople, the general public.	Practitioners working in a certain business, profession, or industry.	Scholars, researchers, or professionals in a particular field of study or discipline.
Information derived from "Is Your Journal Scholarly?", Helmke Library		

Figure 7-3. Audience.

Author

Determining an author's origin and credentials can also help establish what type of source you have.

POPULAR	TRADE/PROFESSIONAL	SCHOLARLY
Often not identified, or a staff journalist or reporter for the publication; credentials usually not given.	Usually, but not always, identified; often a professional or specialist working in the particular field of interest.	Always identified; professional credentials given; contact information often provided.
Information derived from "Is Your Journal Scholarly?", Helmke Library		

Figure 7-4. Authorship.

General Appearance

If you are able to have a copy of the magazine or journal, the appearance of the source itself may give an indicator as to what type of source you have.

POPULAR	TRADE/PROFESSIONAL	SCHOLARLY
Often a slick, glossy, eye-catching cover; color photos; extensive advertising.	Often a glossy cover displaying a professional work environment or a product; usually has color ads and illustrations.	Plain, serious covers; black and white illustrations, charts, and graphs; minimal advertising.
Information derived from "Is Your Journal Scholarly?", Helmke Library		

Figure 7-5. Appearance.

Examples

Here are some examples of each type of journal.

POPULAR	TRADE/PROFESSIONAL	SCHOLARLY
Consumers Digest; Psychology Today; E: The Environmental Magazine; Natural Health; Rolling Stone; Science News.	*Advertising Age; American Libraries; Education Digest.*	*Harvard Environmental Law Review; Journal of Consumer Affairs; Journal of Music Theory; Physics Review.*
Information derived from "Is Your Journal Scholarly?", Helmke Library		

Figure 7-6. Examples.

Locating Popular, Trade/Professional, and Scholarly Sources

You can find all three types of sources in Helmke's databases and indexes.

POPULAR	TRADE/PROFESSIONAL	SCHOLARLY
Use a database that includes a wide variety of general interest magazines such as Academic Search Premier (EBSCOhost).	Use an interdisciplinary database like Academic Search Premier (EBSCOhost), or one focused on a trade or profession such as ABI/Inform Suite for business or ERIC for education.	Use a specialized database geared to a particular field such as PsycINFO (Cambridge Science Abstracts) or Medline (Ovid); other databases that provide a mix of publications may give you an option to limit your search to "peer reviewed," "refereed," or "scholarly" journals.
Information derived from "Is Your Journal Scholarly?", Helmke Library		

Figure 7-7. Locating Sources.

7.3.3 Helmke Databases

Your instructor will most likely introduce you to some of Helmke's databases. However no instructor has enough class time to introduce you to *all* of Helmke's databases. Our library has general, multidisciplinary databases that provide access to books and articles in magazines, newspapers, and journals in a wide variety of subject areas. You may want to explore these first when you start your research as they will give you a broader range

7

of sources. There are also many specialized databases for most subjects taught at IPFW, such as psychology, nursing, education, engineering, history, business, and literature, to name just a few.

Librarians can assist you in using both multidisciplinary and specialized databases. You can begin exploring these on your own by going to the library's website at http://library .ipfw.edu; however, it may be more efficient to email, call, or come to the library to let a librarian help you choose the best databases and formulate a good keyword strategy to identify books and articles on your research topic.

7.4 CITING SOURCES

The citing of source information is standard practice in academic writing and most professional writing. You must cite sources because the ideas in those sources are the *intellectual property* of the writer. In academic circles, failure to cite information is considered plagiarism. In legal circles, it is considered theft by copyright infringement.

Citing sources also serves an important service to the academic community. When you develop a bibliography or works cited list, you give your readers a starting point to find more information on the subject. Readers/researchers can then expand their search further by examining the bibliographies of each of your sources.

TIP: CITATION PAGE GENERATORS
While there are Internet sites that offer citation page generation and programs such as EndNote, which do the same, you should be cautious when attempting to use them. Be sure to check their work or, even better, create your Works Cited or References page on your own.

Scholarly writing has used citation systems since the early 20th century. All citation systems contain some kind of marker in the text that connects the quotation or information from your source to a bibliographic entry for that source. For many years, the standard way to document sources was to insert a number in the text in superscript following the quotation or information (for example, "word"[15]) as a text marker, and put the bibliographic information in a footnote at the bottom of the page or in an endnote at the end of the article. This system is still commonly used in some academic disciplines and by many scholarly journals. The best source for doing this kind of documentation system is *The Chicago Manual of Style*, and some people refer to it as Chicago style, CMS style, or Turabian style (named for the secretary at the University of Chicago Graduate School who developed the system).

In recent years more modern systems have been developed that provide the information without requiring you to constantly jump back and forth between footnotes and the text. There are dozens of these citation systems for specific academic disciplines, but the most common you will encounter in your academic career are the citation styles of the Modern Language Association (MLA style) and the American Psychological Association (APA style).

7.4.1 MLA Citation Style

The MLA generally uses the author's name and page number in parentheses following a quotation, summary, or paraphrase of information from an outside source. For example:

> "The learning history is an emerging genre in business and organizational communication" (Amidon 454).

If the author's name is used in the summary, then the page number is used for the text marker. If the source is a web page without pagination, give a paragraph number (para. 5) instead. For example:

> According to Amidon, learning histories are a new kind of research method and are developing as a writing genre (454).

In the MLA system, you can then find the bibliographic information for the citation by going to the "Works Cited" page, which lists the publication information alphabetically. For example:

Works Cited

Amidon, Stevens. "The Learning History: Analyzing an Emerging Genre." *Journal of Business Communication,* 45 (2008) 451–82.

Bakhtin, Michael. *Speech Genres and Other Late Essays.* Austin, U of Texas P, 1986.

FYI: ITALICS VERSUS UNDERLINING

Some reference books show the titles of songs, books, and films and the names of journals or databases <u>underlined</u> while others show *italics* instead. This is a legacy of the days when people did most of their writing with typewriters, which could not display italics. Underlining was a signal to the typesetter to put the title in italics. Since you are probably writing on a word processing program that can produce italics, you should italicize these titles and names, unless your instructor says otherwise.

7.4.2 APA Citation Style

The APA generally uses the author's name and year of publication in parenthesis following a summary or paraphrase of information from an outside source. The page number is given only if the information is in the form of a direct quotation from the work. For example:

> "The learning history is an emerging genre in business and organizational communication" (Amidon, 2008, p. 454).

7

If the author's name is used in the summary, then the year of publication is used for the text marker. For example:

According to Amidon (2008), learning histories are a new kind of research method and are developing as a writing genre.

In the APA system, you can then find the bibliographic information for the citation by going to the "Reference List" page, which lists the publication information alphabetically. For example:

References

Amidon, S. (2008). The learning history: Analyzing an emerging genre. *Journal of Business Communication*, 45, 451–482.

Bakhtin, M. (1986). *Speech genres and other late essays*. Austin, University of Texas Press.

The APA system includes not only rules for citing sources but also rules for formatting and structuring academic research papers. For more information refer to the latest edition of the *Publication Manual of the American Psychological Association*. More complete guidance can also be found at the Purdue OWL (http://owl.english.purdue.edu/owl).

8

WHAT SHOULD I KNOW ABOUT REVISION AND EDITING?

Threshold Concept

"We all learn that writing is a process, and that revision is an important part of that process. However, many of us still feel disappointed when we produce drafts that are confusing, excessively wordy, and filled with errors in grammar punctuation. We feel as if we have failed, as if we are bad writers. Nothing could be further from the truth! Revision is a good and necessary activity. In fact, it is where most of the best writing occurs!"

If you're stuck on a draft and aren't certain what to change, try some of the revision techniques in this chapter to help you find places in your draft that could benefit from revision.

8.1 DIFFERENCES BETWEEN REVISION AND EDITING

All of the techniques for revising deal, in some way, with your draft as a whole. When you revise, you're looking at elements that affect the entire draft's organization, length, focus, or clarity.

When you edit, you're looking at individual words or sentences. Sometimes, it can be difficult to tell the difference, but as a general rule if you're looking at any of the following you're editing, not revising:

- Typos
- Spelling
- Punctuation
- Grammar errors

8

8.2 REVISION

8.2.1 Revising for Organization

- **Color-code your draft**
  - Decide how many main points you have
  - Get that number of colored pencils or highlighters
  - Assign each point a color
  - Read through your draft highlighting or underlining each sentence (or part of a sentence) with the color that matches the sentence's point
  - Take a look at the colors, cut the paper apart, and group each color together

COMPUTER TIP: COLOR-CODING
You can color-code with a word processor by using the highlight color options. Instead of scissors, use *cut* and *paste* commands to group the colors together.

- **Gloss your draft**

  Glossing is summarizing each paragraph in a piece of writing in one or two words.

  - Read the first body paragraph and decide what the topic of that paragraph is
  - Write the topic in the margins of the draft next to that paragraph
  - Repeat with all of the remaining body paragraphs
  - Read what you wrote in the margins
  - Rearrange your paragraphs so that the same, similar, or related topics are together

COMPUTER TIP: GLOSSING
You can gloss with a word processor by using the comment feature.

- **Check your transitions**

  Transitions are like road signs in your draft. They let readers know where your writing's going next, but they also clarify the connections between ideas.

  - Read through your draft and underline all of your transitions
  - Read the first two paragraphs together
  - Does the transition show the reader the connection between the two ideas?
  - If not, what is that connection?
  - Find a transition that does show the reader how the ideas in those two paragraphs connect
  - Repeat for the rest of the draft

COMPUTER TIP: CHECKING TRANSITIONS
You can mark your transitions by using the underline or highlight features of your word processing program.

8.2.2 Revising for Length

- **Examine your supporting details**

  Often, drafts end up short because the paper makes sense in the writer's head, but that doesn't always mean that it will be clear to a reader. In order to determine if you have enough support to make your points clear, you have to try to think like your reader.

  - Look at the length of each of your paragraphs
  - Is any paragraph less than ½ page long? (An approximate standard length for paragraphs in academic writing is ¾ page)
  - If so, can you add reasons, examples, description, explanation, or analysis to make your point clearer for your readers?
  - If you're having trouble coming up with reasons, examples, description, explanation, or analysis, see "Return to prewriting" below

COMPUTER TIP: EXPANDING YOUR DRAFT

You can examine your supporting details with a word processor by opening a new document and copying and pasting the supporting details of each paragraph into the new document. Then separate each sentence so it starts on its own line. Consider what information you can add under each line.

- **Return to prewriting**

  Sometimes drafts are short because of a lack of ideas. If that's the case, going back to prewriting can help you find additional ideas.

  - Put your draft someplace you can't see it
  - Pick your favorite prewriting technique or a new one and use it
  - Compare your prewriting to your draft to see what new ideas you've uncovered
  - Decide where in your draft those ideas can be added
  - If necessary, repeat

- **Check for wordiness**

  - If your draft is too long, try tightening your writing by getting rid of wordiness
  - Look at your first sentence
  - Are you using phrases that don't add any meaning such as "I think that," "I believe that," or "I feel that"? (Because it's your paper, it's assumed that statements are your own ideas unless you tell the reader otherwise with citation)
  - If so, cross those phrases out
  - Are you telling your readers something they already know?
  - If so, consider cutting that information (If your readers already know it, what's the point of explaining it to them again?)
  - Are there any words or phrases in the sentence that mean the same thing?
  - If so, are they necessary for the sentence's meaning?
  - If not, consider getting rid of the repetitious word or phrase

8

8

- **Narrow your topic**
  - A draft that is too long or too short might mean that you're trying to tackle too much in one paper

If your draft is too long:

- List each of your main points
- Decide which main points are the strongest or the most important
- Are there any main points that aren't as strong or important?
- If so, consider cutting that main point of your draft
- Read your thesis
- Is your topic too big for the size of your paper? (For example, abortion, global warming, or evolution are topics that might reasonably be covered in a book, but not in a paper)
- Read each of your main points by itself
- Could one main point be the topic of your paper?
- If not, talk to your professor or a Writing Center consultant about narrowing your topic

When you try to cover too much in one paper, you can't go into any depth. By making your topic smaller, you actually give yourself more room for depth and detail, both of which add length.

8.2.3 Revising for Focus

- **Check your thesis statement and topic sentences**
  - Underline your thesis statement and each topic sentence
  - Check your first topic sentence to make certain that it clearly connects back to the thesis statement by repeating key words in the thesis
  - If the topic sentence doesn't clearly connect, can you change the wording of either the topic sentence or the thesis statement so that it does clearly connect?
  - If not, consider rewriting the topic sentence
  - If you rewrite the topic sentence, read the entire paragraph to make certain that the paragraph supports the new topic sentence
  - If it doesn't, rewrite the paragraph so that it does support the new topic sentence

COMPUTER TIP: REVISING FOR FOCUS
You can check your thesis statement and topic sentences with a word processor by opening a new document and pasting only the thesis statement and topic sentences into the new document.

- **Gloss your draft**
  - Gloss your draft following the steps under "Revising for Organization"
  - Compare the first paragraph's summary with your thesis statement

- Does the first paragraph's topic clearly connect back to the thesis statement?
- If not, can you rewrite the paragraph so that it does clearly connect?
- If not, consider cutting the paragraph

8.2.4 Revising for Clarity

- **Get rid of second-person pronouns**

  Second-person pronouns are the words "you," "your," or "yourself." Although there are some specific circumstances where second-person pronouns are appropriate and effective, they are most often used as stand-ins for first-person pronouns ("I," "me," "my," or "myself") or refer to people in general. The problem with second-person pronouns is that your reader will not be able to tell if you are referring to you (the writer) or to people in general, and that can create confusion.

  - Read through your draft and circle every second-person pronoun
  - Starting at the beginning, decide who you are actually referring to with the first "you"
  - Replace "you" with the appropriate word
  - If you are referring to people in general, see if there's a more specific word you can use (For example, "you" in this handout refers to people in general, but more specifically, it refers to students or writers. So, if I were to replace "you," I'd use "students" or "writers" instead of "people" or "everyone.")

COMPUTER TIP: SEARCHING FOR PRONOUNS
You can check for second person with your word processor's "find" feature. Open "Find," type in "you," and click "find next." The word processor will automatically take you to the next second-person pronoun in your draft. Replace that pronoun and click "find next" again. Continue until all examples of incorrect pronoun use have been corrected.

- **Check for passive voice and replace it with active voice**

  Passive voice can be confusing for readers because it can hide the subject of the sentence.

  - Read your first sentence
  - Identify the sentence's subject and verb (If it helps, underline them)
  - Is the subject performing the action of the verb?
  - If not, who or what is performing the action?
  - Move the person or object to the front of the sentence (For example, "The paper was written by one student" is in passive voice because the subject, the paper, is not doing the action, writing. The same sentence in active voice would read "One student wrote the paper." Here, the subject, one student, is doing the action, writing.)

8

8

- **Have someone else read your draft**

No matter how closely you go over your own writing, there will most likely be things that are clear to you but not your readers. The best way around this is to have someone else read over your writing. Ask a classmate, a friend, or an instructor, or make an appointment at the Writing Center. To get the most out of your readers, ask questions such as the following:

- Does the organization seem logical? Is there anything that seems out of place?
- Is there anything that you want to know more about?
- Is there anything that you already knew or seems repetitive?
- Is there anything that doesn't make sense to you?

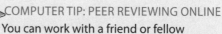 COMPUTER TIP: PEER REVIEWING ONLINE
You can work with a friend or fellow student electronically by emailing your draft as an attachment.

8.3 EDITING

In recent survey research, Dr. Chris Anson of North Carolina State University and Dr. Robert Schwegler of the University of Rhode Island identified ten writing errors that are most likely to confuse or irritate readers.

Some of these errors are grammatical; others are punctuation errors. In learning to identify and correct these ten errors in your own writing, you will be better able to avoid making those mistakes most likely to bother your readers and limit the effectiveness of your writing.

 FYI: GOING BEYOND THE TOP TEN
For a more detailed discussion of sentences, word choice, grammar, punctuation, and mechanics, go to those specific chapters in this handbook.

1. Sentence Fragment

Proofreading symbol: frag

A sentence must have a subject and a verb and must make a complete thought. The following sentence is a fragment because it is missing one of these three criteria.

Faulty sentence:

But I found out about the Writing Center. Which can really help you write better papers.

Corrected sentence:

But I found out about the Writing Center, which can really help you write better papers.

The use of *which* in the second phrase as a subject makes the phrase fragmented. *Which* is never the subject of a statement.

2. Fused Sentence

Proofreading symbol: fs or fused

Two independent clauses (phrases with subject and verbs that can stand alone as a complete sentence) must be connected with a conjunction, separated with a semi-colon, or separated as separate sentences with a period. When they are combined without a conjunction or semicolon, they become "fused" and are often labeled as "run-on" sentences.

Faulty sentence:

> Her teacher marked off points for each grammar error she wanted to be sure she was right.

Corrected sentence:

> Her teacher marked off points for each grammar error, and she wanted to be sure she was right.

The faulty sentence above is missing a comma and a coordinating conjunction (*and*).

3. Comma Splice

Proofreading symbol: cs

Sometimes writers try to separate the clauses of a fused sentence by using a comma (,). A comma is not considered to be a strong enough punctuation mark to separate two independent clauses.

Faulty sentence:

> There seem to be a variety of reasons that students behave in academically dishonest ways, some researchers take the opinion that students don't feel responsible for their actions while others believe that the students do.

Corrected sentence:

> There seem to be a variety of reasons that students behave in academically dishonest ways. Some researchers take the opinion that students don't feel responsible for their actions while others believe that the students do.

4. Unclear Pronoun Reference

Proofreading symbol: ref or pr ref

A pronoun substitutes for a noun that has been previously introduced—its antecedent. When a pronoun gets too far from its antecedent, or when there is more than one possible antecedent, the reader may become confused.

8

8

Faulty sentence:

Removing the probe from the beaker is a delicate task because it can easily break.

Corrected sentence:

Removing the probe from the beaker is a delicate task because the probe can easily break.

Be careful when using pronouns. When in doubt, be specific, even if it causes minor redundancy.

5. Double Negative

Proofreading symbol: dneg or dn

Using two negative terms together confuses the reader. Avoid using more than one negative word such as *no, none, not, never, neither, hardly, scarcely, barely, haven't,* or *don't* in a sentence.

Faulty sentence:

As students enter the university and attend their first classes, they may hear several terms from their instructors they may haven't never encountered before.

Corrected sentence:

As students enter the university and attend their first classes, they may hear several terms from their instructors they may haven't ever encountered before.

You can select the phrase *haven't ever* or *have never* as alternatives, but haven't never is not considered Standard Written English.

6. Dangling Modifier

Proofreading symbol: dm

Pay attention to modifying words or phrases at the beginning of sentences. If the modifier does not mention the person, idea, or thing being modified, readers will expect you to name it as the subject of the main clause that immediately follows. If you fail to do this, you confuse the reader.

Faulty sentence:

While shopping for dog food at the pet store, a Corgi puppy caught my attention.

Corrected sentence:

While I was shopping for dog food at the pet store, a Corgi puppy caught my attention.

7. **Missing or Extra Possessive Apostrophe**

Proofreading symbol: apos

Writers frequently forget to put in an apostrophe (') when using a possessive noun. And sometimes writers put apostrophes into words that aren't possessive.

Faulty sentence:

Academic dishonesty begins quite early in a students academic career.

Corrected sentence:

Academic dishonesty begins quite early in a student's academic career.

Students without an apostrophe indicates multiple students. *Student's* with the apostrophe indicates possession.

8. **Lack of Subject-Verb Agreement**

Proofreading symbol: agr or v agr

Verbs have different forms for the 1st, 2nd, and 3rd person, also for singular and plural subjects. For example, the present tense of the verb *to be* varies with person and number:

I *am*   you *are*   he *is*   we *are*   they *are*

When writers mix up these forms, they confuse the reader.

Faulty sentence:

John are impatient.

Corrected sentence:

John is impatient.

9. **Lack of Pronoun-Antecedent Agreement**

Proofreading symbol: agr or p agr

Nouns are singular or plural in number; so are pronouns. When writers fail to correctly match the two, readers may become confused.

Faulty sentence:

As a student enters the university and attends their first classes, they may hear several terms from their instructors they may not have encountered before.

Corrected sentence option 1:

As students enter the university and attend their first classes, they may hear several terms from their instructors they may not have encountered before.

8

Corrected sentence option 2:

> As a student enters the university and attends his or her first classes, he or she may hear several terms from his or her instructors he or she may not have encountered before.

A *student* is singular and *their* and *they* are plural. To fix the error, change the language so they match. Notice the correct sentence option 1 is less wordy, and, therefore, the better option.

10. Illogical or Inconsistent Shifts

Proofreading symbol: shift

Writers should have a reason when they shift pronouns from one person to another (i.e., from "I" to "he") and when shifting verb tense. When they don't have a reason, readers may become confused.

Faulty sentence:

> I am thinking of buying a house because you built up equity.

Corrected sentence:

> I am thinking of buying a house so I can build up equity.

ASSIGNMENT LINKS 7, 8, AND 9

For example student papers from ENG-W129, ENG-W131, and ENG-W233 see Assignments 7, 8, and 9 in Appendix B of this handbook. These papers have mistakes, so use these papers to practice your editing skills.

9

HOW CAN YOUR COMPUTER MAKE YOUR WRITING CLASS EASIER?

Threshold Concept

"The computer is an awesome tool to help you with your writing. Like any tool, it is only useful if you use it wisely! Because computers allow you to easily edit your papers, it can tempt you to focus on these smaller editing matters, when you should be focusing on revising your draft for purpose, audience, content, and effectiveness."

9.1 MLA AND APA FORMAT

Many instructors ask that your homework be formatted in MLA or APA style. Your course handbook offers examples of MLA- and APA-style papers; Figures 9-1 and 9-2 describe the formatting specifics of the two styles. Make sure you set up the page layout on your word processor to reflect the correct format requirements.

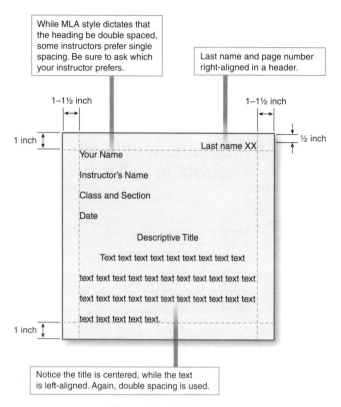

Figure 9-1. MLA Format.

While MLA style dictates that the heading be double spaced, some instructors prefer single spacing. Be sure to ask which your instructor prefers.

Last name and page number right-aligned in a header.

1–1½ inch

1–1½ inch

1 inch

½ inch

Last name XX

Your Name

Instructor's Name

Class and Section

Date

Descriptive Title

Text text text text text text text text text

text text text text text text text text text text text

text text text text text text text text text text text

text text text text text.

1 inch

Notice the title is centered, while the text is left-aligned. Again, double spacing is used.

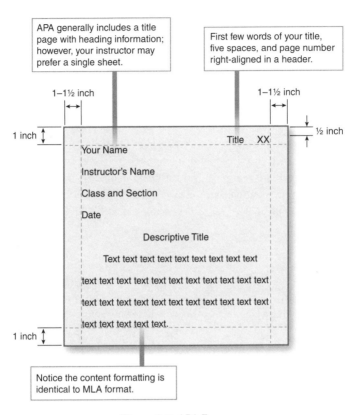

Figure 9-2. APA Format.

COMPUTER TIP: PAGE NUMBERING
When numbering your pages, it's important that you use the page numbering feature of your word processor. If you manually number your pages, you may miss a page change that occurs because of editing or revising.

9.2 MICROSOFT WORD

ITS supports your use of Microsoft Word, which is also the only word-processing program available in computer labs. Because of these facts, many instructors require the use of Microsoft Word **only**. You may purchase the current version of Word at Follett's Bookstore at a reduced student rate.

If you have an earlier version of Word at home, you can visit http://www.microsoft.com to download the Microsoft Office Compatibility Pack, which will allow you to open, edit, and save files using the file formats new to the earlier version.

9

9.2.1 Track Changes

Track changes is a feature in Microsoft Word that allows you, in addition to others, to see your revision process. If your instructor requires that you provide evidence of revision but you don't print a copy of your draft each time you revise, you can use track changes to show your revision process.

9.2.2 Comment

The comment function is roughly equivalent to adding a sticky note or bubble query to a printed document. The function allows you to insert your own comments into some- one else's file (or even into your own) without substantially rewriting the original text. Likewise, it allows others to find your comments quickly. An inserted comment appears on a writer's screen as highlighted text with a bubble attached in the right margin.

9.3 BLOGGING

In order to prepare you for the potential technological components of your career, your instructor may require you to maintain a blog. A blog is an online web log. Some instruc- tors may ask you to keep a blog about your research; some may ask you to document your writing process.

Regardless of your blog topic, it is important to remember that blogs are public. Unless you set the parameters of your blog to private, anyone surfing the Internet may stumble across your blog. Thus, you should not treat a blog as a personal journal, but instead as a piece of writing for public consumption. Be cautious of your language and content; several cases have been brought before the courts for defamation. Similarly, if your classmates will be reading your blog, you should remember to maintain a reasonable tone when discussing potentially upsetting issues, as you don't want to unintentionally offend.

- **To Establish a Blog**
One of the most common free blogging sites is Blogger. To set up a blog in Blogger, follow these steps:

1. Go to http://www.blogger.com
2. Select **Create Your Blog Now**.
3. Enter your Google login or follow the steps to create a Google login.
4. Select a name for your blog. Remember that this name will become part of the URL for your blog, so try to make it unique. You should select the **Check Availability** link to make sure your blog URL is feasible.
5. Choose a template. This will determine the overall look of your blog regarding color, font, and layout.
6. Begin blogging.

9.4 CREATING A WEB PAGE

According to the ITS website, web space is available for individual students to publish noncommercial web pages related to their university responsibilities. Go to the ITS website to find out how to access this web space.

9.4.1 How to Write Web Pages

- On the IPFW campus, there are numerous methods for constructing a web page.
- Dreamweaver is a special software available on the IPFW network used to create a web page.
- Netscape Composer can also be used, although the technology may not be quite as good as Dreamweaver.
- If you already understand HTML code, then you might want to use HomeSite.
- No matter how you create your web pages, you need to understand where to save your pages and how to access your web directory from on campus or from off campus via a browser. Web Page Resources at IPFW offers a lot of basic help.
- The STEPS program offers classes in basic web authoring.

9.4.2 Web Page Design

A web page is like any other type of writing: it has a purpose and audience. Before you begin developing your website, you should consider these points:

- What is your purpose? Are you creating a site to detail your research about breast cancer? If so, then posting pictures of your dogs or kids may not be appropriate.
- What content will you include? Make a list of the content your website needs or should have.
- How will you organize your information? Decide an organizational structure for your website. Consider using a site tree (see Figure 9-3). In this example, the student has one main page with three links: symptoms, treatment, and risk factors. Then each sub page has its own content.
- Depending on the length of the content, there could be sub-sub pages. Mapping out a site tree can help ensure your web page has a logical organizational pattern.
- What colors and fonts do you want to use? There are many color combinations you can use when creating a color scheme for your web page. Consider visiting http://color schemedesigner.com/csd-3.5/ to find a color scheme that works for you. When selecting a font for your web page, pick a font that's clean and simple. Script, balloon, and trendy fonts can be difficult to read or unprofessional. As always, consider your audience and purpose. A trendy font may be appropriate in some genres and not others.

9

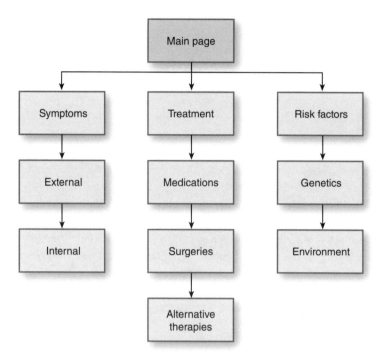

Figure 9-3. Example Site Tree.

10

WHERE CAN I FIND WRITING HELP ON THE WEB?

Threshold Concept

"If you have a question about writing, the first place to look for an answer is the Purdue OWL."

Many Internet sites exist that can help you in your writing endeavors. As you discover what your own writing or grammatical concerns are, you'll want to conduct topic-specific searches using a reputable search engine.

FYI

FYI: WHAT'S THAT URL?

Because of the changing nature of the Internet, it's possible that the URLs listed here may not work. If so, use a search engine like Google to find the proper URL.

10.1 WRITING WEBSITES

- **Purdue OWL**
  Purdue's Online Writing Lab offers a variety of resources to student writers, including over 100 handouts on writing skills you can read, download, or print. They also offer online workshops and podcasts, and they maintain a YouTube channel that hosts videos on different aspects of the writing process and the research process. Visit the OWL at:

  http://owl.english.purdue.edu

- **Elements of Style Online**
  William Strunk Jr.'s famous writing manual is available online. Many instructors recommend you revise your draft using the rules in *EoS*.

  http://www.bartleby.com/141/

10

- **Advice on Academic Writing**
  This website, created by the University of Toronto, offers many links that will aid you as you write in the academy.

  http://www.writing.utoronto.ca/advice

- **Why We Write Series**
  This blog, established during the writer's strike of 2008, is a series of essays by prominent writers of TV and film.

  http://whywewriteseries.wordpress.com

10.2 GRAMMAR WEBSITES

- **Grammar Girl: Quick and Dirty Tips for Better Writing**
  According to its site, "Grammar Girl provides short, friendly tips to improve your writing. Covering the grammar rules and word choice guidelines that can confound even the best writers, Grammar Girl makes complex grammar questions simple with memory tricks to help you recall and apply those troublesome grammar rules."

  http://grammar.quickanddirtytips.com/

- **HyperGrammar**
  The University of Ottawa offers a comprehensive site that allows you to browse various grammatical issues. The site includes both instruction and review exercises.

  http://www.uottawa.ca/academic/arts/writcent/hypergrammar/grammar.html

11

HOW DOES WRITING IN THE BUSINESS WORLD DIFFER FROM COLLEGE WRITING?

Threshold Concept

"Clarity, concision and correctness—the three Cs—are the hallmarks of professional writing. If you want to be respected in your workplace, you need to communicate as professionally as you can. Learn to make your point in clear, understandable language. Learn to get to your point clearly and efficiently. And learn how to eliminate grammar, punctuation, and other mechanical errors in your writing. These kinds of errors are seen as unprofessional in the business world."

Business writing is similar to academic writing. However, it tends to be more formal, it tends to emphasize simpler language when focused on a general business audience, and it is organized around genres, or types of writing, that are different from the typical college paper. Some of these genres are addressed below.

11.1 MEMOS AND EMAILS

Memos and emails are very similar stylistically and are considered the most common form of communication in professional writing. Because of its efficiency and ease, email communication is replacing the printed memo for quick, informal correspondence in the modern workplace.

FYI

FYI: WHAT IS PROFESSIONAL WRITING?

There are many ways to define professional writing. Here we refer to writing done in a workplace setting. Memos, emails, business letters, and reports are types of professional writing most frequently seen in the workplace. IPFW offers several courses you can take to learn more about professional writing. Additionally, we offer a professional writing minor to increase the marketability of your degree as you enter the business world.

HOW DOES WRITING IN THE BUSINESS WORLD DIFFER FROM
COLLEGE WRITING?

11

11.1.1 Content

Memos and emails are considered direct messages: they are straightforward and indicate their purpose immediately. Like most pieces of writing, memos and emails have three main components:

1. Opening—indicate the main purpose of the communication
2. Body—provide details regarding the purpose of the communication
3. Closing—offer any direction or call to action for the intended reader

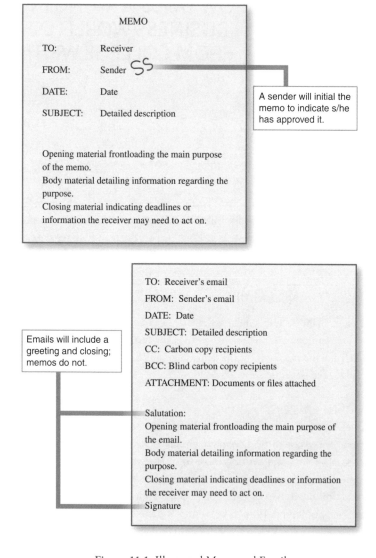

Figure 11-1. Illustrated Memo and Email.

11.1.2 Format

There are only a few formatting differences between email and memo messages as you can see in Figure 11-1.

Figure 11-1 offers you an example of block style. Block style is one of the more common formatting choices in professional writing. Generally block style has the following formatting elements:

- Single-spaced text, double spacing between paragraphs
- Generally no indentation for a new paragraph
- One- to one-and-a-half-inch margins
- Twelve-point font

There are variances in block style. If you're unsure what your instructor wants, it's best to ask.

11.1.3 Email Etiquette

The list that follows gives some basic etiquette suggestions for professional, academic email communication. These have been quoted from emailreplies.com, but you can find helpful tips at http://www.netmanners.com/e-mail-ettiquette-tips/.

What are the etiquette rules?

There are many etiquette guides and many different etiquette rules. Some rules will differ according to the nature of your business and the corporate culture. Below we list what we consider as the 23 most important email etiquette rules that apply to nearly all companies:

1. Be concise and to the point
2. Consider your audience and tone
3. Answer all questions, and preempt further questions
4. Use proper spelling, grammar, and punctuation
5. Do not attach unnecessary files
6. Use proper structure and layout
7. Do not overuse the High Priority option
8. Do not write in CAPITALS
9. Don't leave out the message thread
10. Read the email before you send it
11. Do not overuse Reply to All
12. Take care with abbreviations and emoticons
13. Be careful with formatting

> **TIP: CONSIDER YOUR EMAIL AUDIENCE**
> When sending email to your instructor, pay attention to your tone and writing style. For example, while some instructors may find emoticons humorous, others may find them juvenile. While some may not mind textspeak (LOL, BFF, etc.), others may find it inappropriately informal. When in doubt, maintain a clear, concise, respectful, and professional tone.

11

HOW DOES WRITING IN THE BUSINESS WORLD DIFFER FROM
COLLEGE WRITING?

11

14. Do not forward chain letters
15. Do not request delivery and read receipts
16. Do not copy a message or attachment without permission
17. Do not use email to discuss confidential information
18. Use a meaningful subject
19. Avoid using URGENT and IMPORTANT
20. Avoid long sentences
21. Don't send or forward emails containing libelous, defamatory, offensive, racist, or obscene remarks
22. Don't forward virus hoaxes and chain letters
23. Use the cc: field sparingly

11.2 BUSINESS LETTERS

There are many types of business letters. Business letters can give information, sell a product, deny a request, offer a recommendation, or place an order—to name just a few.

11.2.1 Content

While memos and emails are generally written using a direct pattern, some business letters may be written using an indirect pattern. When your audience may have a neutral or positive reaction to your message, you may select a direct pattern. However, if your audience may have an indifferent or negative reaction to your message, you may want to select an indirect pattern.

DIRECT PATTERN	INDIRECT PATTERN
1. Opening—state your main purpose	1. Opening—use a buffer to ease into the topic
2. Body—provide details	2. Body I—provide reasons for potential bad news
3. Closing—offer direction or action	3. Body II—offer bad news
	4. Closing—offer solution or reconcile bad news to audience

Figure 11-2. Direct and Indirect Pattern.

11.2.2 Format

Figure 11-3 is an example of a full-block style business letter. A business letter has many formatting elements. Notice there is one blank line between the elements of the business letter. However, to make a letter more presentable, you may include more white space between the return and inside addresses.

Return address—the full address of whomever is sending the letter.

Inside address—the full address of the letter's recipient.

Date—the current date, written out in full.

Salutation—a formal greeting. *Dear* is one of the most common salutations.

Letter text—the text of the letter, which should follow the content suggestions in 11.2.1.

Complimentary close—a closing statement. *Sincerely* is a common complimentary close.

Signature block—three to four blank lines to allow for a signature, the typed name, and, if applicable, title or position.

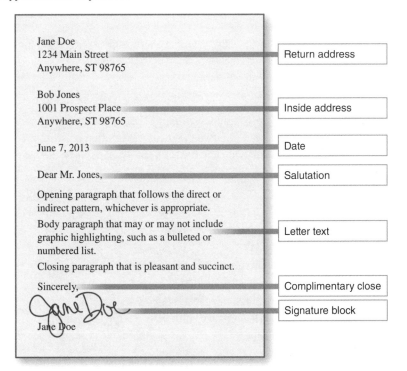

Figure 11-3. Business Letter.

11

HOW DOES WRITING IN THE BUSINESS WORLD DIFFER FROM
COLLEGE WRITING?

11

11.3 EMPLOYMENT COMMUNICATION

Employment communication, particularly your résumé and accompanying cover letter, is arguably the most important written communication you will ever compose. There are many websites, organizations, and services that offer résumé assistance. For example, IPFW Career Services, located in Kettler Hall 109, offers résumé assistance.

11.3.1 Résumés

Many assume the purpose of the résumé is to get you a job; however, the true purpose of a résumé is to get you an interview. The résumé should showcase your skills, education, and experience.

11.3.1.1 Content

You have many options when deciding what to include in your résumé. Ultimately, what you include should be influenced by your audience. Ask yourself the following questions when deciding what to include:

- What does my potential employer need in an employee?
- What job experiences can I highlight that will make me a more appealing applicant?
- Do I have any specific skill sets that I can detail to market myself?

When composing the résumé, do not write in complete sentences; that's what the cover letter is for. Instead, use bullets with action verbs.

You want your résumé to highlight your abilities. Using bulleted statements beginning with an action verb focuses the reader's attention on what you have accomplished and what you can do! Here is a list of some good ones:

Authorized	Determined	Maintained	Revised
Balanced	Developed	Managed	Scheduled
Budgeted	Diagnosed	Marketed	Screened
Built	Directed	Modified	Secured
Changed	Edited	Motivated	Simplified
Constructed	Established	Negotiated	Sold
Contracted	Increased	Operated	Studied
Controlled	Instituted	Produced	Supervised
Coordinated	Interviewed	Purchased	Taught
Created	Introduced	Recommended	Trained
Delegated	Investigated	Reported	Wrote
Designed	Led	Researched	

Figure 11-4. Résumé Action Verbs.

All résumés **must** contain the following information:

- **Heading**—your personal information. Include your full name, home address, home/ cell phone number(s), and email address. You may also include a URL if you have a **professional** website (Twitter and Facebook need not apply). Also, be sure that your contact email is professional; fuzzybunny23@yahoo.com works fine for friends, but shouldn't be how your employers contact you.

The remainder of your résumé can be selected from the sections below. Depending on your experience, education, skills, and the job you're applying for, your selections will vary.

- **Objective**—what your career goal is. This should be specific. *I want a position that will utilize my skills* is too generic. Who *doesn't* want that? If you're strapped for space on the résumé, you can choose to not include an objective.
- **Education**—your educational information. You should include where you went (or are going) to school, your major and minor, and your GPA. You may also include clubs or activities, honors, and pertinent coursework. Unless you've been in high school in the last few years, only include your college information.
- **Work Experience**—your past employment history. You should include the name of your employer, the city and state of employment, the duration of your employment, your position, and your duties. You do not have to include your employer's full address or the name of your supervisor. When listing your duties, be sure to use active verbs.
- **Skills and Abilities**—any skills you have that you didn't gain from your employment. This section sometimes details any computer skills, typing abilities, or general traits that you wish to highlight to potential employers.

Most employers prefer a single page résumé. However, if your work history takes you to a second page, and you have space, the following optional information could be selected to fill space:

- **Clubs or Activities**—your community involvement. If you don't have any work experience in your field, consider including appropriate volunteer work. For example, if you're applying for a lifeguard position, volunteering at the community pool could be considered appropriate experience.
- **Interests**—any applicable interests you have. The key word in this section is *applicable*. Unless you're applying for a position as a ski instructor, no one really cares if you like to ski.
- **References**—your professional references. If you have space, you may include a list of professional or personal references. Do not use family members as references. Consider employers or professors for professional references. Always be sure to ask permission to use someone as a reference.

11

HOW DOES WRITING IN THE BUSINESS WORLD DIFFER FROM
COLLEGE WRITING?

11

11.3.1.2 Format

The visual appeal of a résumé is sometimes just as important as its content. An unappealing or unprofessional résumé may not be read for content at all.

When formatting a résumé, remember to create a professional document by using white space, alignment, tabs, bold, underlining, italics, bullets, and/or numbered lists. Be cautious of overdoing it. Design the page(s) with a good balance of text and white space—not too sparse, and not too busy.

Résumé Tips (for more, see Figure 11-5)

- Be considerate of your readers. Use black ink on white or résumé paper. Try not to use a font smaller than 11 point.
- Be professional. Use a clean font—no script or cartoony bubbles.
- Be consistent with your graphics. If you're going to bold your employers' names, bold them all.
- Pay attention to white space. Just because you have a lot to include doesn't mean your résumé should be all text.
- Respect correctness. **Proofread** your résumé. You don't want to lose an interview because you didn't catch a form/from error.

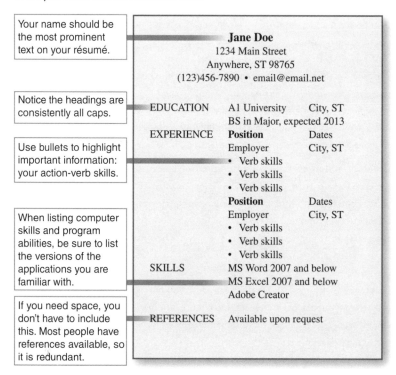

Figure 11-5. Illustrated Résumé.

11.3.2 Cover Letters

The purpose of the résumé cover letter is to highlight and elaborate on information contained in the résumé. The cover letter is formatted like any other business letter.

The content of a cover letter should adhere to the following pattern:

Opening—detail how you heard about the position and clearly state your application for the position. If you know someone who works there, this is the place to drop names.

Body I—detail why you're perfect for the position. You should detail information that's introduced on your résumé, **not duplicate it**. Somewhere in this section, you should refer to your résumé, since the aim here is to connect the company's needs with the skills documented in your résumé.

Body II—detail why you'd like to work *for them*. Visit your potential employer's website and review their mission statement. What about their company appeals to you as a potential employee? **Don't** praise things like vacation time, tuition reimbursement, or hours—that's about *you* not *them*.

Closing—ask for an interview. Thank the potential employer for taking the time to review your application and résumé. You should indicate that you would like to discuss your qualifications further; this hints that there's more to you than what's on the paper. If you ask them to call you, be sure you have a phone number on the cover letter as well as the résumé; sometime the documents get separated.

FYI

FYI: WHY DO I NEED A BODY II SECTION?
Some people call this the "sucking up" section. However, a well-developed Body II paragraph can show your potential employer that you've done your research and are serious about working for them.

11

12

HOW CAN BETTER SENTENCES MAKE MY WRITING CLEARER AND MORE CONCISE?

Threshold Concept

"A sentence requires an actor (the subject), an action (the predicate), and it must make a complete thought. The secret to writing good sentences is to write sentences with engaging actors, active verbs, and clear purposes!"

12.1 ACTIVE AND PASSIVE VOICE

Active sentences are independent clauses with transitive verbs. They follow the basic *subject + predicate* pattern. The difference between active and passive sentences is essentially one of word order. Active sentences follow the pattern of a basic independent clause: *subject + predicate*. That pattern gets reversed in passive sentences.

The assistant weighed the soil samples.

This simple sentence has a subject (S = "The assistant") for a subject, plus a verb (V = "weighed") and a direct object (O = "the soil samples") for the predicate.

If you thought of a sentence in active voice as a kind of equation, it would look like this:

Active Voice = S + V + O

If the sentence were written in passive voice, the order would be reversed:

The soil samples were weighed by the assistant.

Notice that a number of things must happen to convert an active sentence to a passive form:

- The direct object ("the soil samples") must be moved to the beginning of the sentence
- A "to be" verb ("were") must be added before the verb (i.e., "weighed")
- The subject ("The assistant") must be turned into a prepositional phrase beginning with "by" ("by the assistant")
- That prepositional phrase must be moved to the end of the sentence (after the verb)

HOW CAN BETTER SENTENCES MAKE MY WRITING CLEARER AND
MORE CONCISE?

12

If you thought of a sentence in passive voice as a kind of equation, it would look like this:

Passive Voice = O + to be + V + by + S.

Here are a few other examples:

Many parents opt out of certain vaccination programs because of a desire to prevent the development of autism in their children. (Active)

A desire to prevent the development of autism in their children has led many parents to opt out of certain vaccination programs. (Passive)

You should understand the difference between active and passive voice for at least three reasons:

• First, knowing the difference can improve concision (which is the appropriate use of words—not too many and not too few). Notice that sentences in passive voice are more complicated structurally than those in active voice. They're often a bit longer. This is why many composition instructors insist on the active voice; it is simpler and more direct.

• Second, knowing the difference can improve paragraph cohesion (which is the sense a reader gets when a paragraph "flows" from one sentence to another). By being able to rearrange sentences, you're better able to make sure that any given sentence picks up the topic at the end of the preceding sentence. You can also make a conscious effort to begin with a topic that a reader knows and then work toward new information.

• Third, knowing the difference between passive and active voice can help you make conscious decisions about what to emphasize in a sentence. You may have noticed that many in science and technology often prefer the passive voice. This is because they are more interested in what happened, or what was observed, than in who did the observation.

12.2 PARALLEL CONSTRUCTION

Parallel construction should be used when you're listing or clustering items together. Items in your list should be grammatically parallel because it's stylistically more refined and your audience will better comprehend your points.

FYI
FYI: WHAT DOES "GRAMMATICALLY PARALLEL" MEAN?
When all of the items in your list follow the same grammatical structure, they're grammatically parallel. So, if you make a list of nouns with a number of *gerund nouns* (-ing nouns), you should edit your list to ensure all the nouns are in that *gerund* form.

Faulty parallelism:

Beth and I talked for 30 minutes about my organization, ideas, and how I could make my paper longer.

noun — organization   noun — ideas   phrase — how I could make my paper longer

Parallel construction:

Beth and I talked for 30 minutes about my organization, ideas, and paper length.

noun — organization   noun — ideas   noun — paper length

Faulty parallelism:

To be a successful teacher, you need to be knowledgeable, patient, and have boundless energy.

Parallel construction:

To be a successful teacher, you need to be knowledgeable, patient, and energetic.

12.3 CONCISION

Concision involves saying what you mean in an appropriate number of words. When we talk about being concise, we're not talking about eliminating information. Rather, we're talking about expressing that information in an appropriate number of words. The following strategies can help you improve the concision of your writing:

- Eliminate empty words and phrases
  - Wordy: **At this point in time,** enrollment levels **make it impossible** to increase **the number of** teaching positions.

    Notice how the words in bold add little to the meaning of the sentence above.
  - Concise: Enrollment levels prevent us from adding teaching positions.
- Substitute verbs for nouns or adjectives

  Writers create nominalizations when they turn verbs into nouns or adjectives. Consider this list:

VERB	NOMINALIZATION
Investigate	Investigation
Appear	Appearance
Diagnose	Diagnosis
Record	Record
Expect	Expectation
Intervene	Intervention
Direct	Direction
Invent	Invention

Figure 12-1. Nominalizations.

12

HOW CAN BETTER SENTENCES MAKE MY WRITING CLEARER AND
MORE CONCISE?

12

You should learn to spot unnecessary nominalizations because writers often use more words than necessary when they fail to find the best verb for a clause. A good way to avoid this problem is to see whether a sentence could have a stronger verb, which often appears in the sentence already disguised as a nominalization.

- Wordy: The Composition Committee held a discussion of the limitation of class size in ENG-W131.
- Concise: The Composition Committee discussed ENG-W131 class size limits.
- Use "To be" sparingly
  Many writers rely heavily on "to be" verbs (*is, am, are, was, were, be, have been*).

  - Wordy: Many in the medical community believe that this decision is irresponsible; however, it is ultimately the parents who must weigh the pros and cons of vaccinating their baby and make the decision themselves.
  - Concise: Many in the medical community believe that this decision is irresponsible; however, ultimately parents must weigh the pros and cons of vaccinating their baby and make the decision themselves.
- Use "Not" sparingly
  In most cases, the meaning of "not" plus another word can be expressed by a single word.

"NOT" PHRASE	CONCISE EXPRESSION
Not happy	Unhappy
Do not accept	Reject
Not successful	Unsuccessful
Do not care	Indifferent
Not pleased	Displeased
Not complete	Incomplete

Figure 12-2. Eliminating "Not."

To revise the sentences above, remember the basic form of an independent clause: *subject + predicate*. Look for the real predicate. In the last few years, there has been a great debate about vaccinations between the medical community and parents.

- Eliminate overly formal or technical language
  - Wordy: Subsequent to perusing the contractor's RTB (response to bid), Jonathon declared his opposition to their use of SDRAM in the construction of the servers.
  - Concise: After reading the contractor's proposal, John rejected their server design.
- Eliminate excessive metadiscourse
  - Wordy: **As I have already demonstrated**, the history shows that the Russian Futurists, unlike the Futurists in Italy and Great Britain, were more likely to be

Socialists than Fascists. Moreover, **my dissertation documents** the ways in which these differences manifested themselves. **I intend to show that**, in Russia at least, aesthetics and politics were less likely to be conflated, than in Europe.

Notice how this excessive writer's commentary (in bold) adds little to the meaning.

- Concise: History shows that the Russian Futurists, unlike the Futurists in Italy and Great Britain, were more likely to be Socialists than Fascists. Moreover, in Russia at least, aesthetics and politics were less likely to be conflated, than in Europe.

TIP: CONCISENESS
You shouldn't worry about conciseness until after you've written a draft or two of a document. Good prose rarely appears in a first draft. The important thing to remember is to revise what you've already written to make it more concise.

12.4 SENTENCE VARIETY

While repeating key phrases and terms can create unity in your paragraphs, repeating sentence structure can lead to choppy or monotonous prose.

Choppy Prose: Physicists have been studying the nature of matter. They have been doing so for a number of years. They have discovered matter is made up of atoms and even smaller particles. These particles include protons, electrons, neutrons, and other particles. Some of these particles, such as quarks, are strange. The Large Hadron Collider at CERN is expected to find even more of these particles.

By combining sentences, a better variety of simple, compound, and complex sentences leads to fluid prose.

Fluid Prose: Physicists have been studying the nature of matter for a number of years. They have discovered matter is made up of atoms and even smaller particles. These particles include protons, electrons, neutrons, and other stranger particles, such as quarks. The Large Hadron Collider at CERN is expected to find even more of these particles.

TIP: REVISING FOR VARIETY
You shouldn't worry about sentence variety until after you've written a draft or two of a document. Once you've started revising, consider how you've written your sentences. Do you have many simple sentences? Perhaps you can combine some for a more complex sentence structure. Too many complex sentences? Consider placing your most important ideas in simple sentences; audiences pay more attention to and better comprehend simple sentences. An occasional exclamatory sentence (exclamation), imperative sentence (command), or interrogative sentence (question) can also improve sentence variety.

12

12

13

HOW CAN I MAKE MY WRITING BETTER BY MAKING BETTER WORD CHOICES?

Threshold Concept

"The word is one of the smallest units of language, but choosing your words carefully is important. Your decision on what words to use should be based on four factors: (1) does the word express your intended meaning?, (2) is the word audience-friendly?, (3) does the word fit your purpose?, and (4) does the word fit your persona?"

13.1 FORMAL VS. INFORMAL LANGUAGE

Generally, you want to use formal language when writing an academic essay. For example, instead of writing:

That article was totally hard and I didn't understand it at all.

You might write:

The article was difficult to understand.

The use of textspeak, slang, and contractions is generally considered to be informal language. Some instructors also consider the use of *you* as informal language; it's best to check with your instructor to determine his/her perspective on the use of *you* in each writing assignment.

Depending on your audience, it may be more appropriate to use a mixture of formal and informal language in your essay. Again, this decision is something you should discuss with your instructor.

Figure 13-1 below shows some examples of formal vs. informal language.

INFORMAL	FORMAL
so	exceedingly
b/c	because
not real clear	unclear
OK	acceptable
awesome	impressive
have a ball	enjoy
gazillion	many or innumerable
get it	understand

Figure 13-1. Informal vs. Formal Words.

13.2 GENERAL VS. SPECIFIC LANGUAGE

When writing, using specific language is preferable because it helps your audience better understand your point.

For example, if you write *says* when introducing a quote, you've wasted an opportunity to clarify for your reader an author's intent. Instead if you write *contends, argues, asserts, criticizes,* or any variety of verbs that are more specific than *says,* you immediately let your reader know where an author stands within an argument.

GENERAL	SPECIFIC
very good	exceptional, fantastic
someone, they, people	parents, students, John Adams, etc. (Who, specifically, are you referring to?)
stuff, thing	belongings, Star Wars figurine, cell phone, etc. (What, specifically, are you referring to?)
writing instrument	pen, pencil, marker, etc.
put over	install over

Figure 13-2. General vs. Specific Words.

TIP: THE THESAURUS IS YOUR FRIEND, BUT…
When revising, many students will use a thesaurus to "spice up" their language, and to avoid redundant, repeated use of the same word. However, be careful to select a word that is an appropriate synonym for your original word. Also, be careful to select words that most readers will recognize and understand. Sometimes a writer is better off repeating a word than replacing it with an odd word that seems out of place.

13.3 BIASED LANGUAGE

Biased language is offensive and shouldn't be used. Your writing can be labeled biased in many ways, for example, towards gender, age, and ethnicity.

13.3.1 Gender Bias

Use gender-neutral terms when a pronoun is unclear. For example:

A student should watch his language.

In this instance *his* indicates that the student can only be male. To correct the sentence, include the female pronoun as well or make the sentence plural.

A student should watch his or her language.

Students should watch their language.

Avoid dated, gendered terms like those in Figure 13-3.

GENDER BIASED	GENDER NEUTRAL
stewardess, steward	flight attendant
postman	postal worker, letter carrier
chairman	chairperson
male nurse	nurse
policeman	police officer

Figure 13-3. Dated, Gendered Words.

13.3.2 Age Bias

Be respectful when discussing age in your writing. Instead of describing someone as *old/aged* or *childish*, consider using the term *elderly/mature* or *young*. Often, however, including any indication of age is unnecessary.

13

13.3.3 Ethnicity Bias

Be conscientious of labeling and stereotyping when describing ethnicity. For example, *American Indian* is still a commonly used term, but is rapidly being replaced by the term *Native American*. And many Native Americans prefer to be addressed by their tribal names. Furthermore, there are great variances in the use of terms *Chicano*, *Hispanic*, and *Latino*. When in doubt, research which term you should be using. Be conscious that the appropriateness of a given name for an ethnic group may change with time.

13.4 FIGURATIVE LANGUAGE

When writing you can use literal language or figurative language. Literal language refers to words that mean exactly what they say; this type of language is often preferred in academic writing.

Figurative language refers to words that exaggerate or imply alternative meaning. Figures of speech and metaphors, for example, are considered figurative language. When you say *Suzanne was crying crocodile tears*, this figure of speech indicates that Suzanne was simulating distress. When you use figurative language, you risk losing your audience's comprehension; therefore, figurative language must be used very carefully.

13.5 WORD CHOICE AND YOUR PERSONA

Your persona is the role, or character, you assume in your writing. Writing is like a script for a play, and you, the writer, are an actor in that play. Through your choice of words you can come across as a one-sided, mean-spirited person who tries to dominate the audience, or you could choose words that present you as reasonable and open-minded. You can write like a robot, or you can write as if you are a bundle of emotions. You can write like a specialist, or you can write like a well-informed citizen. You get to choose the kind of role you want to play in your text!

14

HOW CAN I RECOGNIZE AND CORRECT GRAMMAR ERRORS?

Threshold Concept

"The most common grammatical errors involve the misuse of verbs or pronouns. The best way to avoid these errors is to (1) keep a mental or physical list of the errors you make; (2) learn how to identify these errors while proofreading; and (3) develop strategies for correcting these errors. Eventually this process will be internalized, and you will find that you are making this kind of error less frequently."

14.1 PARTS OF SPEECH

In order to discuss some rules of grammar, it's important that you know the basic parts of speech. The examples of the parts of speech are italicized below.

- **Noun**—a person, place, thing, or idea
  It seems that it is easier to find *research* to support *vaccinating* your *child* than not.
- **Verb**—an action or state of being
  It *seems* that it *is* easier to find research to support vaccinating your child than not.
- **Pronoun**—takes the place of a noun
  So in a writing class, academic honesty then can be defined as using *your* own thoughts and words or giving credit to the thoughts and words of others.
- **Adjective**—describes a noun
  So in *a writing* class *academic* honesty then can be defined as using your *own* thoughts and words or giving credit to *the* thoughts and words of others.
- **Adverb**—describes a verb, adjective, or other adverb
  One of their biggest arguments is that children are given *too* many vaccinations today.
- **Preposition**—shows relationship between two or more words
  The book had fallen *behind* the bookcase.

14

- **Conjunction**—joins words, phrases, and clauses
  Ultimately, it seems that academic honesty *and* academic dishonesty are two topics that create great debate amongst professors, *but* there isn't really clear agreement as to its definition *or* its causes.

14.2 VERBS

14.2.1 Subject Verb Agreement

Subjects and verbs should always match.

For example, singular subjects have singular verbs:

Beth is very kind and helpful. (*is* vs. *are*)

Similarly, plural subjects have plural verbs:

Some professors take the dishonesty personally. (*take* vs. *takes*)

When subjects are joined by *either/or* or *neither/nor* the verb should match the subject that is closest to it:

Neither the online consultants nor the Center is available on Saturdays.

Neither the Center nor the online consultants are available on Saturdays.

Because *Center* is singular, *is* is the appropriate verb. However, if the order is rearranged, *consultants* would require *are*, the plural verb.

Indefinite pronouns require singular verbs:

Some argue that you should…

Subjects and verbs should be located closely together for the sake of clarity. When they are separated, errors can happen.

Faulty sentence:

There seem to be a variety of reasons that students behave in academically dishonest ways…

Corrected sentence:

There seems to be a variety of reasons that students behave in academically dishonest ways…

In this case, *a variety* is the singular subject (not *reasons*), thus the verb should be *seems*.

14.2.2 Irregular Verbs

Another common verb error is the incorrect use of an irregular verb. English has many verb tenses; we will focus on the three most commonly used tenses: present, past, and past participle.

PRESENT	PAST	PAST PARTICIPLE
Today I _____.	Yesterday I _____.	I have _____ in the past.

Figure 14-1. Verb Tenses.

Regular verbs, such as *to walk*, add an *–ed* to the end of the verb to create a past or past participle tense:

PRESENT	PAST	PAST PARTICIPLE
Today I walk.	Yesterday I walked.	I have walked in the past.

Figure 14-2. Regular Verbs.

Irregular verbs, on the other hand, do not follow such a consistent pattern. Figure 14-3 lists the most commonly misused irregular verbs. The eleven verbs listed, according to the Lancaster-Bergen corpus, account for nearly 50 percent of the irregular use in the U.S.

PRESENT	PAST	PAST PARTICIPLE
Come	Came	Come
Find	Found	Found
Get	Got	Got, Gotten (U.S.)
Give	Gave	Given
Go	Went	Gone
Know	Knew	Known
Make	Made	Made
Say	Said	Said
See	Saw	Seen
Take	Took	Taken
Think	Thought	Thought

Figure 14-3. Some Common Irregular Verbs.

14

14.3 PRONOUNS

14.3.1 Pronoun and Antecedent Agreement

The noun that the pronoun refers to is called its antecedent. Pronouns should have a clear antecedent that matches in both gender and number.

- **Clarity**

  Often, an antecedent can be vague or unclear. Specifically, watch out for the words *it*, *this*, *that*, *these*, and *those* followed by verbs.

  Faulty sentence:

  > You can go into the Center and use their computers to work on your papers, but you can't use them for just anything like in a regular lab; it has to just be your papers.

  Corrected sentence:

  > You can go into the Center and use their computers to work on your papers, but you can't use the computers for just anything like in a regular lab; you can just work on your papers at the Center.

  Here the use of *it* and *them* can cause confusion for the readers between the references to the writer, the Writing Center, and the Writing Center's computers. When in doubt, be specific.

- **Number**

  Singular antecedents require singular pronouns, and plural antecedents require plural pronouns.

  Faulty sentence:

  > As a student enters the university and attends their first classes, they may hear instructors use several terms they may haven't never encountered before.

  Corrected sentence option 1:

  > As students enter the university and attend their first classes, they may hear instructors use several terms they may have never encountered before.

  Corrected sentence option 2:

  > As a student enters the university and attends his or her first classes, he or she may hear instructors use several terms he or she may have never encountered before.

  A student is singular and *their* and *they* are plural. To fix the error, change the language so they match. Notice the correct sentence option 1 is less wordy and, therefore, the better option.

- **Gender**

  As to not offend or confuse your readers, pronouns should match their antecedents in gender. Be careful to keep a clear antecedent.

Faulty sentence:

> Theresa Smith, an IPFW freshman, said that she used the drop-in consulting to answer a comma question. Her teacher marked off points for each grammar error, and she wanted to be correct.

Corrected sentence:

> Theresa Smith, an IPFW freshman, said that she used the drop-in consulting to answer a comma question. Her teacher marked off points for each grammar error, and Smith wanted to be correct.

FYI: ISN'T "HE" A GENDER-NEUTRAL PRONOUN?

Back in the day, *he* was considered an appropriate pronoun to use if the gender was unclear or neutral; however, some readers may find this usage sexist. Your best bet if you have a gender or gender-neutral antecedent is to make it plural; the pronoun *they* offends no one.

In this example, *she* could refer to either the student or the instructor (as the instructor's gender is not specified). When in doubt, restate the antecedent for the sake of clarity.

14.3.2 Pronoun Case

There are three main pronoun cases: objective, subjective, and possessive. Depending on what function the pronoun serves in the sentence you're writing, the case will vary. *This, that, these, those,* and *which* do not change case.

SUBJECTIVE	OBJECTIVE	POSSESSIVE
I	Me	My/Mine
You	You	Your/Yours
He, She, It	Him, Her, It	His/Her/Hers/It/Its
We	Us	Our/Ours
They	Them	Their/Theirs
Who	Whom	Whose

Figure 14-4. Pronoun Case.

14

14

Most native English speakers can hear when they use the wrong case. *"Him is going to the store"* shouldn't sound correct. However, there are special instances in which pronoun case can get tricky.

FYI: GRAMMAR CHANGES

You may notice that the sentence "You gave it to who?" doesn't sound bad, even though the objective case of the pronoun should be "whom." That is because the use of "whom" as the object case of "who" is gradually disappearing from the language. This is another case of language evolving over time. However, you should probably use "whom" in this case, rather than "who," since most grammar books still teach "whom" as the correct use for the objective case of this pronoun.

When *and* is used, you can easily select the wrong case. To solve this dilemma, remove the *and* phrase from the sentence, and check your pronoun case.

Faulty sentence:

> Send the report to Bob and I.

Corrected sentence:

> Send the report to Bob and me.

If you remove *Bob and* from the sentence, the proper pronoun choice is clear. *Send the report to I* uses the incorrect case and sounds awkward.

When a pronoun follows any form of the verb *to be*, select the subject case.

> It is she who should be concerned.

FYI: ISN'T IT ALWAYS "AND I"?

While our third-grade English teachers drilled the "So-and-so and I" rule into our noggins, the rule doesn't always work. "And I" follows the case rules just like other pronouns. If the expression is being used as a subject, "John and I" is correct. If it's being used as an object of a verb or preposition, "John and me" is correct.

Another time the pronoun case rules become difficult is when making comparisons with *than* or *as*. When in doubt, rearrange your sentence.

Faulty sentence:

> She believes in capital punishment more than him.

Corrected sentence:

> She believes in capital punishment more than he.

To better understand these case rules, it's important to finish the thought. The faulty sentence implies that she believes in capital punishment more than she believes in him. The corrected sentence fulfills the author's intent: she believes in capital punishment more than he does.

Who vs. *Whom*: Sometimes the best way to decide whether you should use *who* or *whom* is to replace the *who/whom* with *he/him*. If *he* is appropriate, choose *who*. If *him* is appropriate, choose *whom*. For example:

> She will bring whomever she wants.

In this instance, you would say she will bring *him*, so *whom* becomes the correct choice.

14.3.3 Collective Pronouns

Collective pronouns refer to a large group or organization such as *team*, *committee*, *family*, or *group*.

These antecedents also generally require singular pronouns. For example:

> The Writing Center offers lots of services. Handouts is one of *its* services.

Because *its* refers back to the Center as a whole (because the Center as an entity offers handouts), the singular pronoun is appropriate.

However, there are instances in which a collective antecedent can have a plural pronoun. For example:

> The Writing Center offers lots of services. Consulting with students is *their* biggest service.

Because *their* refers, indirectly, to the Center's staff (as they are the ones who consult with students, not the Center as an entity), *their* is appropriate.

14.3.4 Indefinite Pronouns

Some pronouns aren't clearly singular or plural and, thus, create agreement issues.

- **Singular**
  another, anybody, anyone, anything, each, either, everybody, everyone, everything, little, much, neither, nobody, no one, nothing, one, other, somebody, someone, something

  For example:

  > Somebody hit me. (*hit* vs. *hits*)

- **Plural**
  both, few, many, others, several

  For example:

  > Many are coming to dinner. (*are* vs. *is*)

14

14

- **Singular or Plural**

    all, any, more, most, none, some

TIP: PRONOUN AGREEMENT

For pronouns that can be singular or plural, look to identifiers within the context of the sentence for agreement clues.

15

HOW CAN I RECOGNIZE AND CORRECT PUNCTUATION ERRORS?

Threshold Concept

"Punctuation does two things. First, a punctuation mark acts like a traffic cop, or a traffic sign, directing the reader to take some action. Second, it acts like an orchestra conductor, controlling the rhythm of your language. By reading your writing out loud during the proofreading stage, you can usually identify the need for punctuation."

15.1 THE PERIOD (.)

15.1.1 End of a Sentence

The period acts like a stop sign. Use a period to indicate the end of a sentence.

15.1.2 Polite Request

Use a period to end a polite request. While the sentence may be structured as a question, the writer intends that the audience will comply with his/her request. For example:

> Will you send me the forms immediately.

COMPUTER TIP: WORD PROCESSING THE PERIOD

When using a typewriter, the common rule was to insert two spaces after a period. However, with the word processor taking over the job of the typewriter, this rule has changed. A single space after the period is considered acceptable now, and in many cases is preferred.

15.2 THE QUESTION MARK (?)

Use a question mark to end a query. For example:

> How can parents be expected to make such a decision?

15

If you're tagging a question at the end of a statement, do not forget to separate the question tag with a comma. For example:

They are being unreasonable, right?

The use of multiple question marks to provide emphasis is considered informal and not recommended for academic or professional writing.

15.3 THE EXCLAMATION POINT (!)

Use an exclamation point to indicate strong feelings or excitement. For example:

You won't regret it!

Exclamation points can be considered juvenile or informal by many instructors; use them sparingly, if at all, in academic writing.

15.4 THE COMMA (,)

The comma acts like a flashing yellow light. It is telling you to slow down, but continue moving.

15.4.1 Introductory Words or Phrases

Commas are required after introductory words, phrases, or clauses. For example:

Even though I'm tired, I intend to finish my work.

15.4.2 Restrictive and Nonrestrictive Clauses

Use a comma to set off nonrestrictive clauses only. For example:

Theresa Smith, an IPFW freshman, said that she used the drop-in consulting to answer a comma question.

The phrase *an IPFW freshman* is not imperative to the meaning of the sentence, thus, can be set off with commas.

FYI

FYI: RESTRICTIVE CLAUSES VS. NONRESTRICTIVE CLAUSES

A restrictive clause contains information that is imperative to the meaning of the sentence. A nonrestrictive clause contains information that adds to the sentence but does not affect the true meaning of the sentence.

15.4.3 Compound Sentences

Use a comma to separate two independent clauses that are joined by a coordinating conjunction—*for, and, nor, but, or, yet,* and *so.* The acronym FANBOYS can be used as a memory aid. For example:

> So, it seems that students are not only being given bad examples of academic honesty, but they also consider that honesty is no longer a black-and-white issue and is instead many shades of gray.

The two sentences before and after *but* are independent sentences. The best way to test the sentences quickly is to read them aloud separately. If they make sense, they're most likely independent sentences.

15.4.4 Items in a Series

Use a comma to separate items in a series of three or more. For example:

> They're men, women, young, old, students, and former students.

FYI

FYI: COMMA BEFORE THE *AND* IN A LIST
Always include a comma before the *and* when separating items in a list of three or more. It's a convention of journalistic writing to remove the final comma in a series; however, in your English classes, you should follow Standard Written English, which dictates that the final comma be included.

15.4.5 Other Comma Rules

- Use commas to set off the year if the month and date are included. For example:

> January 20, 1994, is my birthday.

- Use commas to set off the state, county, or country if it follows a city. For example:

> She's traveling to Mobile, AL, next week.

15.4.6 Common Comma Errors

- **Separating a Subject and Its Verb**

  Unless the comma is being used with a nonrestrictive phrase, you should never separate a subject and its verb with a comma. For example:

> You should go to the Writing Center, because it has a good location, good consultants, a lot of availability, and lots of services.

- **Items in a List**

  Do not use a comma if your list only contains two items.

- **Independent Clause Followed by Dependent Clause**

  If your dependent clause follows your independent clause, the comma is unnecessary.

15

15

15.5 THE SEMICOLON (;)

The semicolon acts like a flashing red light. It is telling you to stop briefly, and then start moving again.

15.5.1 Separating Independent Clauses

Use a semicolon to separate two independent clauses.

Faulty sentence:

> You can go into the Center and use their computers to work on your papers; but you can't use the computers for just anything like in a regular lab.

Corrected sentence:

> You can go into the Center and use their computers to work on your papers; you can't use the computers for just anything like in a regular lab.

The use of the coordinating conjunction *but* causes a grammatical error. Remember, you use commas with coordinating conjunctions to connect two independent sentences.

15.5.2 Items in a List

Use a semicolon to separate items in a list that already contain commas themselves. This provides clarity for your reader. For example:

> The hours are: Mon., Tues., Wed., Thu. 10 a.m.–6 p.m.; Fri. 10 a.m.–2 p.m.; and Sun. 1–5 p.m.

?

TIP: WHY USE A SEMICOLON?
You can show your reader that the ideas in the two sentences you've connected are related. Additionally, using a semicolon is a good way to create sentence variety in your writing.

15.6 THE COLON (:)

The colon is like a road sign listing the restaurants at the next exit. What follows a colon is added information.

15.6.1 To Illustrate

Use a colon after a complete sentence to directly relate the material following the colon to the previous sentence. For example:

> Most professors, however, still hold to the black-and-white perspective: there is no "little bit" or "kinda" when it comes to academic honesty.

The colon indicates that the writer will explain what the black-and-white perspective is.

Do not use a colon after the following terms: *includes, including, to be* verbs, *such as.*

Faulty sentence:

> The hours are: Mon., Tues., Wed., Thu. 10 a.m.–6 p.m.; Fri. 10 a.m.–2 p.m.; and Sun. 1–5 p.m.

Corrected sentence:

> The hours are Mon., Tues., Wed., Thu. 10 a.m.–6 p.m.; Fri. 10 a.m.–2 p.m.; and Sun. 1–5 p.m.

15.6.2 In Salutations

Use a colon in the salutation of a business letter. For example:

> Dear Mr. Smith:

15.6.3 In a Title

Use a colon to separate a main title from a subtitle.

> Bob Costas: A True Broadcasting Everyman

15.7 THE APOSTROPHE (')

15.7.1 Possession

- Use an apostrophe to show possession in a singular noun.
  Faulty sentence:

  > Academic dishonesty begins quite early in a students academic career.

  Corrected sentence:

  > Academic dishonesty begins quite early in a student's academic career.

Students without an apostrophe indicates multiple students. *Student's* with the apostrophe indicates possession.

- Use an apostrophe to show possession in a plural noun. For example:

  > But maybe we can agree at least that we can try to broaden students' perspectives and raise their standards, so that they can be better critics—and better self-critics.

FYI: MISSING OR EXTRA APOSTROPHES
While failing to provide an apostrophe to show possession when needed seems like a small error, research shows that this error tends to annoy readers as much or more than more serious grammatical errors. The same holds true for adding an apostrophe when it is not needed.

Because the perspectives belong to multiple students, the apostrophe goes after the *s*.

15

- Use an -'s at the end of the second item when indicating joint ownership.
  Mary and Suzy's bistro

This example indicates that the bistro is jointly owned by Mary and Suzy.

- Use an -'s at the end of each item when showing two or more separate owners.
  Tom's and Frank's bistros

This example indicates that Tom and Frank each *individually* own a bistro.

- Do not use an apostrophe when using possessive pronouns.
  Faulty sentence:

    Academic honesty and it's cousin plagiarism are two terms that students should become familiar with in their college career.

  Corrected sentence:

    Academic honesty and its cousin plagiarism are two terms that students should become familiar with in their college career.

15.7.2 Omission

- Use an apostrophe to show omission of letters, as in contractions; however, many instructors frown on the use of contractions in formal, academic writing. For example:

    After looking at the IPFW statement on academic honesty it's clear that cheating is considered academic dishonesty, but what else falls under that umbrella?

- Use an apostrophe to show omission of letters, as in abbreviations. For example:

    'Twas the night before Christmas

The apostrophe in this situation replaces the *I* of "It was."

15.7.3 Other Uses

- Use -'s to make lowercase letters, abbreviations with periods, and example words plural. For example:
    She finds there are too many b's in the nursery rhyme.

- Do not use an apostrophe to make numbers or capital letters plural. For example:
    She hopes that she earns As on all her tests.

    He was fond of music from the '80s.

15.8 QUOTATION MARKS (" ")

15.8.1 Quoted Material

Use quotation marks to indicate quoted material. Quotation marks must **always** work in pairs. If you have open quotation marks, you **must** have closing quotation marks. Also, quotations within quotations use single quotation marks.

FYI: BEGINNING AND ENDING QUOTES WITH ELLIPSES
Generally, it's unnecessary to begin or end a quote with ellipses. It is assumed by your reader that there is material both before and after your quote.

Faulty quotation:

> Thompson writes, "The college freshman sitting across from me in my office looked me in the eye and insisted vehemently that he didn't know why his paper was a word-for-word rendition of its twin, which I had found on the Web and was holding next to his own. Another student, having waited 3 days until I returned his graded essay—a cut-and-paste collage of several Web sources labeled "final"—assured me that he had simply given me an incorrect draft. A third brought his mother to the conference; it turned out that not only had she prepared the paper for him, but she also had done the plagiarizing (2439).

Corrected quotations:

> Thompson writes, "The college freshman sitting across from me in my office looked me in the eye and insisted vehemently that he didn't know why his paper was a word-for-word rendition of its twin, which I had found on the Web and was holding next to his own. Another student, having waited 3 days until I returned his graded essay—a cut-and-paste collage of several Web sources labeled 'final'—assured me that he had simply given me an incorrect draft. A third brought his mother to the conference; it turned out that not only had she prepared the paper for him, but she also had done the plagiarizing" (2439).

15.8.2 Irony
Use quotation marks to indicate irony sparingly, as it's commonly considered informal use. Quotation marks to emphasize information is generally frowned upon; instead try bold or italics.

Faulty sentence:

> Most professors, however, still hold to the black-and-white perspective: there is no "little bit" or "kinda" when it comes to academic honesty.

Corrected sentence:

> Most professors, however, still hold to the black-and-white perspective: there is no *little bit* or *kinda* when it comes to academic honesty.

15.8.3 Terminology
Use quotation marks when referring to a term. Some texts also indicate single quotes are more acceptable for this function.

15

15.8.4 Titles

Use quotation marks for titles of the smaller parts of whole items: article titles, songs, television episodes, book chapters, etc.

Faulty Sentence:

> However, in *Immunisation: Are Parents Making Informed Decisions?* Marfe contends…

Corrected sentence:

> However, in "Immunisation: Are Parents Making Informed Decisions?" Marfe contends…

TIP: THE PART OF A WHOLE RULE
When deciding if something should be underlined or italicized in MLA formatting, follow this rule: parts of things are in quotes; whole things are underlined or italicized. For example, an article in a magazine is in quotes; the magazine itself would be underlined or italicized. The title of a song from a record album would be in quotes; the title of the album would be underlined or italicized.

15.9 THE HYPHEN (-) AND DASH (–, —)

Hyphens and dashes are like arrows or detour signs. They point you in the right direction, or tell you to take a detour, and then continue on.

15.9.1 Hyphens (-)

The hyphen is visually shorter than the dash. Use a hyphen when expressing a compound modifier. For example:

> I suppose we could just view anti-plagiarism instruction as a necessary evil, not particularly educational in the positive sense, but necessary.

When listing hyphenated material, suspend the hyphen. For example:

> The benefits are available for full- and part-time employees.

COMPUTER TIP: WORD PROCESSING HYPHENS AND DASHES
The hyphen can be found on most computer keyboards. It is usually located to the right of the "0" above the alphabet. The en dash can be created on most computers by holding down the ALT key and simultaneously typing "0150" on the numeric keypad. The em dash can be created by typing two hyphens and then hitting the ENTER key.

15.9.2 The En Dash (–)

The en dash is visually longer than the hyphen and shorter than the em dash.

The most common use of the en dash is to indicate periods of time in place of the word *through*. For example:

> He was a professor at IPFW from 2003–2012.

Additionally, the en dash is used when combining an open compound. For example:

The town is located near the Michigan–Indiana border.

The NCTE conference is a joint high school–college conference.

15.9.3 The Em Dash (—)

The em dash is the most common form of the dash. Use an em dash to emphasize information. For example:

What's most astounding, though—and most insulting—is that students plagiarize in ways that are so easy to catch.

15.10 PARENTHESES ( )

Parenthetical marks are always used in pairs; if you open parentheses, be sure to close them.

- Use parentheses to de-emphasize information. For example:
  The instructions (see page 10 of your booklet) will detail how to select the proper insurance program for your family.

- Use parentheses to indicate in-text citations. For example:
  Many students who cheat blame faculty for their transgressions, especially professors who fail to respond to what students consider obvious incidents of cheating that occur in their courses (McCabe and Trevino, 2002).

15.11 BRACKETS [ ]

Like parentheses, brackets are used in pairs. Never open a bracket without closing it.

- Use brackets to clarify information within a quote.
- Use brackets for information within parentheses.

FYI: WHAT'S [SIC]?
The bracketed term [sic] within a quote means "thus in the original." It is used to clarify to a reader that an error in a quote is the original author's error, not yours. You should never correct an error in a quotation—quote precisely, even if the quotation contains an error.

15

15

15.12 ELLIPSES (…)

Use ellipses to indicate material has been removed from a quote. Remember that even though you're removing material, you should still maintain the author's original intent. For example:

> Some students complain that their professors are cheating them by spending more time consulting and publishing than teaching or preparing for classes. … Notwithstanding outside influences, cheating is strongly dependent on what occurs in the classroom, and the biggest factor is the instructor.

15.13 THE SLASH [/]

The slash is considered standard usage in composition; however, the backslash is not—it's best to never use the backslash.

Use the slash to connect words of equal value (*and/or, he/she*). There should be no spaces before or after the slash.

16

HOW CAN I RECOGNIZE AND CORRECT MECHANICAL ERRORS?

Threshold Concept

"We all make the occasional error in spelling or capitalization. Our errors will be less noticeable to our readers if we at least make sure we spell and capitalize in a consistent manner."

16.1 CAPITALIZATION

16.1.1 The First Word in a Sentence
The first word of a sentence is always capitalized. For example:

Academic honesty and its cousin plagiarism are two terms that students should become familiar with in their college career.

16.1.2 Proper Nouns and Adjectives
Proper nouns and proper adjectives are always capitalized. For example:

The Writing Center is conveniently located.

Capitalization is not necessary if the writer is not referring to a specific writing center.

16.1.3 Titles of Documents
Titles of printed works are capitalized except for conjunctions, articles, and prepositions of four or fewer letters. For example:

However, in "Immunisation: Are Parents Making Informed Decisions?" Marfe contends…

16.1.4 Professional Titles
Capitalize professional titles if they precede a person's name. Examples include:

Instructor Smith, Reverend Thomas, Professor Martin

16.1.5 Poetry

Capitalize the first letter of a line of poetry. For example:

There is a place where the sidewalk ends/ And before the street begins,/ And there the grass grows soft and white,/ And there the sun burns crimson bright,/ And there the moon-bird rests from his flight/ To cool in the peppermint wind.

16.1.6 Specific Names or Titles

Capitalize the specific name of a course, flight, gate, etc.; however, do not capitalize the general description. For example:

My ENG-W129 instructor said in class that it's better to go in person than online.

16.2 NUMBER USE

16.2.1 Numbers Expressed as Words

16.2.1.1 Ten and Under

Generally, the numbers ten and under are expressed as words. For example:

Academic honesty and its cousin plagiarism are two terms that students should become familiar with in their college career.

16.2.1.2 Beginning a Sentence

When a number begins a sentence, it is expressed as a word. For example:

Fifty-four of the documented cases were imported from other countries, and 63 of the 64 measles patients had never been vaccinated against the disease.

16.2.2 Numbers Expressed as Numerals

16.2.2.1 Numbers Over Ten

Generally, numbers over ten are expressed as numerals. For example:

Federal health officials who track measles cases declared the United States virtually free of the disease in 2000, with yearly reported cases between 2000 and 2007 ranging from 29 to 116.

If a sentence contains numbers that can be expressed as either numerals or words, select one and be consistent.

16.2.2.2 Specific Situations

When using technical terms, dates, addresses, and measurements, numbers should be expressed as numerals. For example:

The research findings showed that 40 percent of almost 50,000 undergraduates questioned have plagiarized from the Net, up from only 10 percent in 1999.

16.3 SPELLING

A quick Google search of "commonly misspelled words" will result in many such lists. It behooves you to become familiar with the words you frequently misspell.

Often misspelling is the result of using an incorrect word. For example, their/there, weather/whether, and its/it's. Spell-checkers will not catch this type of spelling mistake. When in doubt, check the dictionary.

COMPUTER TIP: FIND AND REPLACE WORDS

You can use Microsoft Word's Find and Replace feature to quickly select and replace any words you have misspelled multiple times in your document.

16

16

A

APPENDIX A:
HANDOUTS

APPENDIX A TABLE OF CONTENTS

A

HANDOUT 1: GENERIC ASSIGNMENT TEMPLATE

This handout will help you ask the right kinds of questions when your instructor gives you a writing assignment orally.

Instructor _____

Class_____

Due Dates: _____

Rough Draft: _____

Final Draft: _____

Other Due Dates:

_____

_____

_____

Formatting:

- MLA or APA _____
- Length _____
- Font/Font Size _____
- Spacing _____

Sources:

- Type Accepted _____
- Number _____

Other Specifications:

_____

_____

_____

A

A

HANDOUT 1: GENERIC ASSIGNMENT TEMPLATE

This handout will help you ask the right kinds of questions when your instructor gives you a writing assignment orally.

Instructor _____

Class_____

Due Dates: _____

Rough Draft: _____

Final Draft: _____

Other Due Dates:

_____

_____

_____

Formatting:

- MLA or APA _____
- Length _____
- Font/Font Size _____
- Spacing _____

Sources:

- Type Accepted _____
- Number _____

Other Specifications:

_____

_____

_____

A

A

HANDOUT 1: GENERIC ASSIGNMENT TEMPLATE

This handout will help you ask the right kinds of questions when your instructor gives you a writing assignment orally.

Instructor _____

Class_____

Due Dates: _____

Rough Draft: _____

Final Draft: _____

Other Due Dates:

_____

_____

_____

Formatting:

- MLA or APA _____
- Length _____
- Font/Font Size _____
- Spacing _____

Sources:

- Type Accepted _____
- Number _____

Other Specifications:

_____

_____

_____

A

A

HANDOUT 1: GENERIC ASSIGNMENT TEMPLATE

This handout will help you ask the right kinds of questions when your instructor gives you a writing assignment orally.

Instructor _____

Class_____

Due Dates: _____

Rough Draft: _____

Final Draft: _____

Other Due Dates:

_____

_____

_____

Formatting:

- MLA or APA _____
- Length _____
- Font/Font Size _____
- Spacing _____

Sources:

- Type Accepted _____
- Number _____

Other Specifications:

_____

_____

_____

A

A

HANDOUT 1: GENERIC ASSIGNMENT TEMPLATE

This handout will help you ask the right kinds of questions when your instructor gives you a writing assignment orally.

Instructor _____

Class_____

Due Dates: _____

Rough Draft: _____

Final Draft: _____

Other Due Dates:

_____

_____

_____

Formatting:

- MLA or APA _____
- Length _____
- Font/Font Size _____
- Spacing _____

Sources:

- Type Accepted _____
- Number _____

Other Specifications:

_____

_____

_____

A

A

HANDOUT 2: WRITING CENTER PRE-CONSULTATION REFLECTION

This handout will help you prepare for your consultation.

Instructor _____

Class_____

When is your assignment due? _____

What instructions have you been given for the assignment?

_____

_____

_____

What kind of help do you need?

__ Understanding the assignment   __ Sentence structure and clarity

__ Generating ideas/getting started   __ Writing an introduction or conclusion

__ Generating a thesis statement   __ Building an argument

__ Integrating sources   __ Citations in APA or MLA style

__ Document design or format   __ Supporting ideas with evidence

__ Other, you specify:

_____

_____

Tell us, in your own words, what you most want to focus on:

_____

_____

_____

_____

_____

_____

A

A

HANDOUT 2: WRITING CENTER PRE-CONSULTATION REFLECTION

This handout will help you prepare for your consultation.

Instructor _____

Class _____

When is your assignment due? _____

What instructions have you been given for the assignment?

_____

_____

_____

What kind of help do you need?

___ Understanding the assignment

___ Generating ideas/getting started

___ Generating a thesis statement

___ Integrating sources

___ Document design or format

___ Other, you specify:

___ Sentence structure and clarity

___ Writing an introduction or conclusion

___ Building an argument

___ Citations in APA or MLA style

___ Supporting ideas with evidence

_____

_____

Tell us, in your own words, what you most want to focus on:

_____

_____

_____

_____

_____

_____

A

A

HANDOUT 2: WRITING CENTER PRE-CONSULTATION REFLECTION

This handout will help you prepare for your consultation.

Instructor _____

Class _____

When is your assignment due? _____

What instructions have you been given for the assignment?

_____

_____

_____

What kind of help do you need?

__ Understanding the assignment   __ Sentence structure and clarity

__ Generating ideas/getting started   __ Writing an introduction or conclusion

__ Generating a thesis statement   __ Building an argument

__ Integrating sources   __ Citations in APA or MLA style

__ Document design or format   __ Supporting ideas with evidence

__ Other, you specify:

_____

_____

Tell us, in your own words, what you most want to focus on:

_____

_____

_____

_____

_____

_____

A

A

HANDOUT 2: WRITING CENTER PRE-CONSULTATION REFLECTION

This handout will help you prepare for your consultation.

Instructor _____

Class_____

When is your assignment due? _____

What instructions have you been given for the assignment?

_____

_____

_____

What kind of help do you need?

__ Understanding the assignment   __ Sentence structure and clarity

__ Generating ideas/getting started   __ Writing an introduction or conclusion

__ Generating a thesis statement   __ Building an argument

__ Integrating sources   __ Citations in APA or MLA style

__ Document design or format   __ Supporting ideas with evidence

__ Other, you specify:

_____

_____

Tell us, in your own words, what you most want to focus on:

_____

_____

_____

_____

_____

_____

A

A

HANDOUT 2: WRITING CENTER PRE-CONSULTATION REFLECTION

This handout will help you prepare for your consultation.

Instructor _____

Class _____

When is your assignment due? _____

What instructions have you been given for the assignment?

_____

_____

_____

What kind of help do you need?

__ Understanding the assignment   __ Sentence structure and clarity

__ Generating ideas/getting started   __ Writing an introduction or conclusion

__ Generating a thesis statement   __ Building an argument

__ Integrating sources   __ Citations in APA or MLA style

__ Document design or format   __ Supporting ideas with evidence

__ Other, you specify:

_____

_____

Tell us, in your own words, what you most want to focus on:

_____

_____

_____

_____

_____

_____

A

A

HANDOUT 2: WRITING CENTER PRE-CONSULTATION REFLECTION

This handout will help you prepare for your consultation.

Instructor _____

Class_____

When is your assignment due? _____

What instructions have you been given for the assignment?

_____

_____

_____

What kind of help do you need?

__ Understanding the assignment   __ Sentence structure and clarity

__ Generating ideas/getting started   __ Writing an introduction or conclusion

__ Generating a thesis statement   __ Building an argument

__ Integrating sources   __ Citations in APA or MLA style

__ Document design or format   __ Supporting ideas with evidence

__ Other, you specify:

_____

_____

Tell us, in your own words, what you most want to focus on:

_____

_____

_____

_____

_____

_____

A

A

HANDOUT 3: ENGLISH DEPARTMENT GRADE APPEALS GUIDELINES

In considering whether to appeal a course grade, you should analyze the situation carefully to be sure you have both appropriate grounds and adequate evidence.

The grounds for making a successful appeal are listed in IPFW's *Undergraduate Bulletin*. They are "prejudice, caprice, or other improper condition such as mechanical error." In this context, "prejudice" means that the instructor based your grade on a personal reaction to you, rather than on the merit of your work. "Caprice" means that the instructor based your grade on some improper factor, for example the day of the week or the toss of a coin, rather than on the merit of your work. An improper condition might be, in addition to mechanical error, an unannounced deviation from a grading system printed in the syllabus or a clearly unreasonable requirement, such as attending events scheduled during your other classes. Note that simple disagreement with the instructor about the quality of your work, even if other readers agree with you, is not a valid ground for appeal, nor is the possibility that you might have done better work with a kinder or more conscientious instructor.

In addition to having an appropriate ground for appeal, you must be able to cite evidence to support your claims. If you find yourself saying, "I think," "I feel," or "I believe," you may simply be presenting your opinion rather than evidence that will lead an impartial party to agree with you. Likewise, asserting that someone who is not present believes something or heard something will probably carry little weight. Written evidence, for example, copies of the syllabus, assignments, evaluation sheets, and your graded papers, may be valuable. Also, witnesses may meet with the department's Grade Appeals Committee or provide written statements. The committee will certainly weigh the validity and relevance of all the evidence presented to it.

After having spoken with your instructor to clarify any aspects of the grade that either of you might not understand, if you are still unsatisfied and wish to pursue an appeal, you should write a letter to the Department Grade Appeals Committee stating what you think your grade should be, explaining the grounds for your claim and summarizing the evidence that supports it. Include your phone number and times when you can be reached and are generally available for appointments. You should attach statements and copies of other written evidence. Be sure that this letter and its attachments present all of the evidence that supports your appeal. Either take this material to the department office, CM 145, or send it to the address below:

Chair, Grade Appeals Committee
Department of English and Linguistics
Indiana University–Purdue University Fort Wayne
Fort Wayne, IN 46805-1499

A

The Chair of the committee will make your materials available to committee members and will contact you to see whether you would like to meet with the committee. The committee may ask you for more information or for further explanation, and it may contact the instructor for a statement or to ask specific questions. Whether you meet with the committee or not, the Chair of the committee will let you know the committee's recommendation by mail.

B

APPENDIX B:
ASSIGNMENTS AND
EXERCISES

APPENDIX B TABLE OF CONTENTS

B

ASSIGNMENT 1: FRAMEWORK CONNECTION

After reviewing the IPFW Baccalaureate Framework and the outcomes for your writing course, write a two-paragraph essay describing how you see the connection between your writing class and the IPFW Baccalaureate Framework.

ASSIGNMENT 2: THE APPEALS

The appeals are used in all kinds of writing and speech. Select a piece of persuasive non-fiction. Read it and identify how the author uses the appeals to influence his/her audience.

B

B

ASSIGNMENT 3: GENRES

Try to fill in the matrix below. For example, one genre of writing that occurs in a working context that aims to persuade an investor to provide capital for a new business is a "Business Plan."

	School Context	Working Context	Public Context	Personal/ Everyday Context
Informative Aim				
Persuasive Aim		**Business Plan**		
Interpretive Aim				
Expressive Aim				

ASSIGNMENT 4: CONTENT ANALYSIS

For this paper, you will compare and contrast the views of growth and change found in "The Achievement of Desire" and *A Hope in the Unseen*. Discuss the argument these texts make regarding the impact of education on an individual's growth and change. Do they suggest that education does or does not change a person? Do they disagree about the emotional consequences of education? What is their view of the impact of schooling on family relations? Do they agree on some points, but not on others? These are only some of the questions you could consider as you write this essay; *you do not have to write about all of them.*

You should, however, integrate your own opinion into this essay. What do you think of these texts' arguments? If you think both texts make similar arguments, do you agree with their conclusions? If the texts' arguments diverge, which one do you find yourself agreeing with more?

This project must be four–five pages long and typed, using 12-point Times New Roman font and MLA format. A draft must be ready for peer review on the date I specify and a draft (with all previous work attached) will be turned in to me at the beginning of class one week later. I will respond to your draft and return it to you with comments. You will then revise your draft and submit it for grading (again, with all previous work attached) on a due date of your choice, but no later than specified on the syllabus.

(This assignment was developed by Dr. Sara Webb-Sunderhaus)

B

B

ASSIGNMENT 5: RHETORICAL ANALYSIS

For this paper you will write a rhetorical analysis of a complex nonfiction text. You should address all of the following issues as they apply to the text you have chosen.

THE **CONTEXT** OF THE ISSUE(S): Identify the issue(s) with a brief summary of the text.

THE **CLAIM**: What is the writer arguing, and what kind of evidence is being used to support the argument?

THE **"CALL"** TO WRITE: Identify the sense of urgency. Why write now?

THE **WRITER'S** CREDENTIALS: Include (if available) the writer's education, experience, credentials, awards, affiliation, reputation, prior publication, etc.

THE **PUBLICATION** INFORMATION: In addition to the publication's name and the date published, include (if available) the publisher's affiliation (commercial, academic, institutional, governmental, religious) as well as its stated or identifiable political, social, cultural, economic, and/or religious philosophy/ideology.

THE WRITER'S **PURPOSE**: State whether to inform, explain, persuade, entertain, and/ or call to action.

THE WRITER'S **RELATIONSHIP** TO THE READER (AUDIENCE): Identify the intended reader(s), i.e., specific and/or general audience.

THE AUTHOR'S USE OF **LANGUAGE**: Include specific examples of connotation/ denotation, language patterns, figures of speech, etc. Discuss tone (attitude—objective, critical, passionate, curious, entertaining, casual, formal, patronizing, amusing, angry, sarcastic, etc.).

THE **EFFECTIVENESS** OF THE TEXT: State the effectiveness of the text in influencing the thoughts of its intended audience. Give specific examples from the text that support the conclusions of your analysis.

This project must be four–five pages long and typed, using 12-point Times New Roman font and MLA format. A draft must be ready for peer review on the date I specify and a draft (with all previous work attached) will be turned in to me at the beginning of class one week later. I will respond to your draft and return it to you with comments. You will then revise your draft and submit it for grading (again, with all previous work attached) on a due date of your choice, but no later than specified on the syllabus.

ASSIGNMENT 6: GENRE ANALYSIS

For this paper you will compare and contrast two scholarly articles in an attempt to explore the genre. You should address all of the following organizational structures for your analysis.

Introduction
- Start with a brief discussion of the subject/topic that the two articles are exploring.
- State the thesis, either implied or stated, in each article.

Audience and Purpose Questions
- Who is the intended audience/community for each article?
- What is the audience likely to know? Want to know? Why?
- How much time will the audience spend with the information presented in the articles?
- What is the purpose of the information presented in the articles? (Inform, persuade, and/or entertain?)
- What are the significant similarities and/or differences between the audiences of the two articles? (Comparison/Contrast)

Rhetorical Issues: Ethos, Pathos, and Logos
- How does each article help to establish the information's credibility? Is it effective?
- How does each article help to evoke an emotional response from the audience? Which emotions? Why?
- What types of evidence are used to support the claims of the information in the articles? Is it appropriate? Why or why not?
- What are the significant similarities and/or differences between the ways ethos, pathos, and logos are used in the two articles? (Comparison/Contrast)

Structure
- How is the information shaped by the article(s)? (Consider the limitations/freedoms of space, time, layout, audience, and so on.)
- How are the articles organized to convey their messages? (Consider strategic layout, design, and organization of visuals and text.)
- What are the significant similarities and/or differences between the structures of the two articles? (Comparison/Contrast)

Style/Language
- How formal/informal is the language?
- What specialized vocabulary is used?
- What other communication features (i.e., visuals, colors, fonts, etc.) contribute to the message?
- What are the significant similarities and/or differences between the language and style of the two articles? (Comparison/Contrast)

B

B

Conclusion/Synthesis

- Which article was more effective in conveying its message? Why?
- Offer a final comment on the impact of scholarly genres on academic discourse.

References

- Be sure to list your two genres using APA citation format.

This project must be four–five pages long and typed, using 12-point Times New Roman font. A draft must be ready for peer review on the date I specify and a draft (with all previous work attached) will be turned in to me at the beginning of class one week later. I will respond to your draft and return it to you with comments. You will then revise your draft and submit it for grading (again, with all previous work attached) on a due date of your choice, but no later than specified on the syllabus.

ASSIGNMENT 7: EDITING A W129 STUDENT PAPER

The following student paper has numerous errors. Read the paper and circle all the errors you can find. Use proofreading marks where you know them.

ENG-W129 Example Essay

The following is an essay for a W129 course. The student was asked to write an evaluation essay that met the following criteria:

- Establishes criteria and states a judgment for each criterion
- Offers at least three (3) primary sources to support judgments
- Organizes the material presented in a coherent, logical manner
- Describes the topic being evaluated
- Maintains a focus toward the specified audience throughout the essay
- Uses the conventions of an academic essay and standard written English

B

From: Suzy Student

To: Instructor Smith, ENG W129

Date: October 15, 2009

Subject: Writer's Memo

My Rhetorical Situation: I want to persuade IPFW students to go to the Writing Center with their papers. I'm using a persuasive tone and the essay genre.

What I'm Comfortable With: I think my information is pretty solid. I got a lot of good information from my interview.

What Areas Need Work and My Plan to Address Them: I think my first draft sounds too rough. I mostly just wrote stuff using my own language, but when I read it, it sounds choppy and repetitive. I'm going to work on combining my sentences and varying my words.

Questions for My Reader

1. I used some stuff from the Writing Center's website. I know we can only use primary stuff, but is that ok?

2. Are my topic sentences too repetitive?

Student 1

Suzy Student

Instructor Smith

ENG W129

October 15, 2009

The Writing Center

Allot of students have a hard time writing papers. Sometimes it's because they don't like it. Sometimes it's because it's hard for them. I have a hard time writing papers myself. But I found out about the Writing Center. Which can really help you write better papers. One of the things I like best about the Writing Center is it's on campus and that makes going there easy. Another thing I like about the Writing Center is the people who work there are nice and don't make fun of me if I don't have a lot of my draft done, they just help me make it stronger. You should go to the Writing Center, because it has a good location, good consultants, a lot of availability, and lots of services.

The Writing Center is conveniently located. To find the Writing Center, you just have to go to the basement of Kettler. It's in KT G19, right by CASA, down the hall from the common area on the Subway side. Lots of students hang out there to study, so if you want to just pop in sometime to have a question answered, that's really convenient. Also since it's by CASA everything you may need to get help with your classes is all in one place. They call it "The Spot." Elizabeth Keller, a consultant at the Writing Center for three years, says, "I think the location is okay. However, I would much prefer the Writing Center to be elsewhere (like the library), for example." She said she wants "More room to spread out with students, more room to have group consultations, and more room to help with multimedia students.

B

B

Wherever the location may be, I want it to be HUGE. And with lots of ways for students to express themselves, whatever that may be." Overall, I give the Writing Center's location an A.

Another reason to go to the Writing Center is the consultants. There are many consultants who are available to help you at the Writing Center. I met with Keller to talk about the Writing Center. We talked about my paper for Sociology. Beth and I talked for 30 minutes about my organization, ideas, and how I could make my paper longer. Beth was very kind and helpful. I was kinda afraid she might boss me around but instead she understood the problems I was having and made some really good suggestions. Keller said, "For the last 3 years, I've been a peer consultant. That is, I work with students, one on one, helping them with any part of their writing process (getting started, understanding the assignment, revising what they already have, etc.)." There are about 15 consultants at the Writing Center. They're men, women, young, old, students, and former students. I like that there's a good variety of people who work there. So if you want to get lots of different suggestions, you can meet with lots of different consultants. The consultants get an A.

The availability at the Writing Center is excellent. The Center is open on Sunday through Friday. The hours are: Mon., Tues, Wed, Thu. 10 a.m.– 6 p.m.; Fri. 10 a.m.–2 p.m.; and Sun.1–5 p.m. The Center is also open for drop-in consultations if you didn't make an appointment or if you only need a quick question answered.

Theresa Smith, an IPFW freshman, said that she used the drop-in consulting to answer a comma question. Her teacher marked off points for each grammar error and she wanted to be sure she was right. She said, "It was nice to have someone who knows for sure tell me I was right." The Center also offers online consulting. It's available Mon.–Fri. 10 a.m.–6 p.m., but is closed weekends, breaks, and holidays. My English W129 instructor said in class though that it's better to go in person than online. Neither the online consultants nor the Center are available on Saturdays. Because of that, I give the availability an A–.

The Writing Center offers lots of services. Consulting is their biggest service. Keller said, "When I meet with a student, I want to help them do three things: First, I want them to feel comfortable in sharing their writing. I've found that through safe conversation, even the most reluctant or confused student can understand the things that he/she is at the Writing Center for. Secondly, I will do whatever I can as a consultant to show them how to communicate effectively. [I removed stuff here, how do I show my readers that?] it is my hope that the student will see me as an extension of the classroom; we often have copies of their textbooks, etc. that we use during a consultation. And third, I want the student to walk away with something…anything! [I removed stuff here too.] My main goal (especially if this is a student's first visit) is to show the student that writing isn't a mystery; writing is a great way to convey ideas, to convince people of things, and above all to express how they feel." The consultants can help with any writing project—not just stuff for English class.

The Writing center also offers other services. Their website has many handouts that students can use like "Writing a Thesis Statement and Opening Paragraphs," "Annotating a Text," and "Commas." They also offer workshops during the semester. My favorite service (other than the

B

consulting) is the computers that they have in the Writing Center. You can go into the Center and use their computers to work on your papers; but you can't use them for just anything like in a regular lab, it has to just be your papers. So, if you're working on a paper and have a quick question, you can ask the desk consultant. Usually he is available to answer any questions you might have. Because the Writing Center has so many great services, it gets an A.

The Writing Center is a great place to go because of it's location, it's consultants, it's availability, and it's services. According to their Website, "The mission of the IPFW Writing Center is to help writers learn to use language more effectively, produce clear writing appropriate to their purposes and audiences, and develop positive attitudes about writing and about themselves as writers." The Writing Center meets that mission. Every IPFW student who has to write a paper should go the Writing Center for feedback. You won't regret it!

ASSIGNMENT 8: EDITING A W131 STUDENT PAPER

The following student paper has numerous errors. Read the paper and circle all the errors you can find. Use proofreading marks where you know them.

ENG-W131 Example Essay

The following is an essay for a W131 course. The student was asked to write an evaluation essay that met the following criteria:

- Informs the reader about an academic issue
- Organizes the information in a logical manner
- Remains a descriptive paper with a moderately neutral tone
- Maintains a focus toward the audience throughout the essay.
- Uses the conventions of an academic essay and standard written English
- Uses three (3) or more sources (including two print) documented appropriately in MLA style

B

From: Thomas Student

To: Instructor Smith, ENG W131

Date: October 15, 2009

Reflective Cover Letter

Instructor Smith and W131 Peers:

I want to inform my audience about the issue of academic honesty. I'm using a neutral, reasoned tone and the academic essay genre.

This is the second draft of my essay. I mostly worked on organizing my points. I've added headings to help my readers follow my organizational pattern. When I took this draft to the Writing Center, the person told me that I may be quoting too much. But I really like all my quotes. Can you help me figure out which I can summarize or paraphrase?

I worked really hard on my Works Cited page. Can you look at it to see if it's right?

For my next draft, I want to try to change some of my quotes to my own words. I also think that I should keep working on my organization.

Student 1

Thomas Student

Instructor Smith

ENG W131

October 15, 2009

Academic Honesty: Student and Professor Perceptions

As a student enter the university and attend their first classes, they may hear several terms from their instructors they may haven't never encountered before. Academic honesty and it's cousin plagiarism are two terms that students should become familiar with in their college career. According to the IPFW website, "Academic honesty is expected of all students. You are responsible for knowing how to maintain academic honesty and for abstaining from cheating, the appearance of cheating, and permitting or assisting in another's cheating" ("Academic Honesty" par 1). While it's clear students are expected to have academic honesty, what *exactly* it is can be confusing to students. A lot has been said about academic honesty, by both students and professors. This paper will attempt to investigate student and instructor perceptions and definitions of academic honesty.

Defining Academic Honesty

After looking at the IPFW statement on academic honesty it's clear that cheating is considered academic dishonesty, but what else falls under that umbrella? Well, according to Wikipedia, "Academic dishonesty or academic misconduct is any type of cheating that occurs in relation to a formal academic exercise. It can include:

Student 2

- Plagiarism: The adoption or reproduction of ideas or words or statements of another person without due acknowledgment.

- Fabrication: The falsification of data, information, or citations in any formal academic exercise.

- Deception: Providing false information to an instructor concerning a formal academic exercise—e.g., giving a false excuse for missing a deadline or falsely claiming to have submitted work.

- Cheating: Any attempt to give or obtain assistance in a formal academic exercise (like an examination) without due acknowledgment.

- Sabotage: Acting to prevent others from completing their work. This includes cutting pages out of library books or willfully disrupting the experiments of others" (par 1).

So in a writing class academic honesty then can be defined as using your own thoughts and words or giving credit to the thoughts and words of others.

But amongst students there seem to be degrees of academic honesty. Carol Thompson states that, "Clearly, students are having chances aplenty to see their elders act dishonestly; it should not be surprising that the students interviewed by Kate Zernike (2002) for the New York Times asserted that using a paragraph without attribution did not constitute cheating; echoing the physicians above, 45% said "falsifying lab or research data" did not constitute cheating (p. A10)" (2441). Similarly, Elliot Levy and Carter Rakovski found that students believed the following:

The highest degree of dishonesty was attached to stealing an exam, submitting another's paper, copying an exam with or without the other student's knowledge, copying a paper or project, allowing someone to submit one's work, using a crib sheet, and allowing another to copy an exam. The lowest level of dishonesty was giving and receiving help on graded material, copying and allowing someone to copy homework, copying from the internet without giving the source, and allowing use of one's paper not knowing that it would be submitted by another student (743).

So, it seems that students are not only being given bad examples of academic honesty, but they also consider that honesty is no longer a black and white issue, but many shades of gray.

Most professors, however, still hold to the black and white perspective: there is no "little bit" or "kinda" when it comes to academic honesty. Thompson writes, "The college freshman sitting across from me in my office looked me in the eye and insisted vehemently that he didn't know why his paper was a word-for-word rendition of its twin, which I had found on the Web and was holding next to his own. Another student, having waited 3 days until I returned his graded essay—a cut-and-paste collage of several Web sources labeled "final"—assured me that he had simply given me an incorrect draft. A third brought his mother to the conference; it turned out that not only had she prepared the paper for him, but she also had done the plagiarizing (2439).

But professors do seem to struggle with how to address the problem of academic dishonesty in their classrooms. William Badke says, "Education is supposed to be a positive experience. That makes droning on to a room full of students or researchers about the evils of plagiarism essentially anti-educational, as important as the topic may be. It hearkens back to high school when we were shown films of automobile accidents and their victims to scare us into being safe drivers. I suppose we could just view

B

anti-plagiarism instruction as a necessary evil, not particularly educational in the positive sense, but necessary" (59). So instead of becoming the hardnosed lecturer as Badke mentions, Jonathan Malesic thinks that professors should do the following:

By showing our students what good work is, helping them discover what makes it good work, and explaining how we can very clearly tell the difference between good and bad work, or the relative differences between two authors, we are not only improving their minds, but improving their "natures." That is a lofty word, one that even humanities professors (maybe especially humanities professors) hesitate to utter. But maybe we can agree at least that we can try to broaden students' perspectives and raise their standards, so that they can be better critics—and better self-critics (par 15).

Frequency of Academic Dishonesty

Academic dishonesty begins quite early in a students academic career. Levy reports that, "A survey by the Josephson Institute of Ethics found that 74% of the 12,000 high school students polled had cheated on a test at least once in the past year. The same survey also indicated that students are more likely than in the past to lie to parents and teachers and even to steal (Taylor, 2003). More than 35% of high and middle school students agreed with the statement "I would be willing to cheat on a test if it would help me get into college" (Gomez, 2001)" (736). Badke also claims that "Cut-and-paste plagiarism from the Internet is increasing, according to the 2005 study from The Center for Academic Integrity (www.academicintegrity.org/cai_research. asp). The research findings showed that 40 percent of almost 50,000 undergraduates questioned have plagiarized from the Net, up from only 10 percent in 1999. What is more, fully 77 percent did not view such activity as a serious issue" (58).

Reasons for Academic Dishonesty

There seem to be a variety of reasons that students behave in academically dishonest situations, some researchers take the opinion that students don't feel responsible for their actions while others believe that the students do. For example, Levy claims that:

Many students who cheat blame faculty for their transgressions, especially professors who fail to respond to what students consider obvious incidents of cheating that occur in their courses (McCabe and Trevino, 2002). Students who perceive that their peers cheat and are not penalized cheat more (Bowers, 1964; McCabe and Trevino, 1993, 1997). Some students complain that their professors are cheating them by spending more time consulting and publishing than teaching or preparing for classes (Fishbein, 1993). ...Notwithstanding outside influences, cheating is strongly dependent on what occurs in the classroom and the biggest factor is the instructor.

Lower levels of cheating have been observed when students believe that cheaters will be caught. And, if students perceive that cheating is likely to be reported, they are also likely to believe that cheaters will be caught and punished (McCabe et al., 2001a, b). (737–738). Malesic says, "There are probably dozens of reasons why some students plagiarize. They're lazy. They're afraid. They perceive plagiarism to be standard practice. They believe that any means to a good grade are legitimate. What's most astounding, though—and most insulting—is that students plagiarize in ways that are so

B

Student 6

easy to catch. They cut and paste without thinking to cover their tracks. They copy from the most obvious sources possible. They find and replace words and then do not proofread to ensure clarity" (pars. 9 and 10). Badke is more forgiving when he says, "To be charitable, many people have no idea they are committing plagiarism. They use sources carelessly or falsely believe that information can be appropriated at will. One person's plagiarism is another person's research, isn't it? If it's on the Net and it's free to use, why can't I just copy and paste it?" (58).

Some professors take the dishonesty personally; they think the student's cheating is a personal diss. Lang argues, however, "That the last thing on the student's mind, when he made the poor decision to plagiarize, was his personal relationship with you. He did it because he was lazy, or he was rushed for time, or he felt overwhelmed by the assignment. He did not do it to send any message to you about your worth as a teacher, or to test your integrity, or to make your life miserable. He did it for his own reasons and did not expect to be caught, and hence thought little, or not at all, about how his actions would affect you" (par 15). He continues, "When my students violate academic honesty, they are not sinning against me; they are sinning against the standards of an intellectual community they have agreed to join. The proper response is to follow the standards that the community has established for such offenses" (Lang par 18).

Other professors blame our culture for the rise in academic dishonesty. Willen says, "McCabe's comments cited in the *Times* article, though, suggest one way that we might begin to think about it. He explains that "undergraduates say they need to cheat because of the intense competition to get into graduate school, and land the top jobs." The need that students express should not be taken lightly. Surprisingly, McCabe indicates that this need is not an effect of the expectations or requirements for courses being unreasonable; nor are the pressures created by workloads, deadlines and poor time management the primary issues. Instead, this need reflects an anxiety about the future, an anxiety reinforced by their experiencing higher education as professional preparation that is a highly competitive, high stakes endeavor" (56).

Willen also goes on to state, "In this climate what counts most are numbers and results, and those who get results, those who make the grade, regardless of how they go about doing it, reap the benefits. As Callahan suggests, the fact that opportunities for graduates are becoming more limited; that the middle class in American society is shrinking; that the rewards for coming out on top seem astronomical (think for instance of CEO salaries), it is not surprising that, when faced with a choice between preserving one's integrity or doing what is unethical but may ensure some measure of success or security, many students will choose the latter" (56).

Conclusion

Ultimately, it seems that academic honesty and academic dishonesty are two topics that create great debate amongst professors, but there isn't really clear agreement as to its definition or is causes. Malesic points out the irony of academic dishonesty:

The paradox of plagiarism is that in order to be really good at it, you need precisely the reading and writing skills that ought to render plagiarism unnecessary. If my students could recognize what differentiates their own

B

Student 8

writing styles from those of authors whose work they find online, then they should also be able to perform with ease all the tasks I require for their essay assignments: to read texts carefully, to determine the relative importance of textual evidence, to formulate a clear thesis, and to defend it convincingly. (par 19) **75**

Works Cited

"Academic Dishonesty." Wikipedia. 31 July 2008.
    <http://en.wikipedia.org/wiki/Academic_dishonesty>.

"Academic Honesty." IPFW Policies and Regulations. 31 July 2008.
    <http://www.ipfw.edu/academics/regulations/honesty.shtml>

Badke, William. "Give Plagiarism the Weight It Deserves." Online 31.5 (Sep. 2007):
    58–60. Academic Search Premier. EBSCO. Helmke Library, Fort Wayne, IN.
    31 July 2008. <www.lib.ipfw.edu>.

Lang, James M. "It's Not You." Chronicle of Higher Education 54.9 (26 Oct. 2007):
    78–78. Academic Search Premier. EBSCO. Helmke Library, Fort Wayne, IN.
    31 July 2008. <www.lib.ipfw.edu>.

Levy, Elliott S., and Carter C. Rakovski.. "ACADEMIC DISHONESTY: A Zero
    Tolerance Professor and Student Registration Choices." Research in Higher
    Education 47.6 (Sep. 2006): 735–754. Academic Search Premier. EBSCO.
    Helmke Library, Fort Wayne, IN. 31 July 2008 . <www.lib.ipfw.edu>.

Malesic, Jonathan. "How Dumb Do They Think We Are?." Chronicle of Higher
    Education 53.17 (15 Dec. 2006): C2–C3. Academic Search Premier. EBSCO.
    Helmke Library, Fort Wayne, IN. 31 July 2008. <www.lib.ipfw.edu>.

Thompson, Carol C. "Unintended Lessons: Plagiarism and the University." Teachers
    College Record 108.12 (Dec. 2006): 2439–2449. Academic Search Premier.
    EBSCO. Helmke Library, Fort Wayne, IN. 31 July 2008. <www.lib.ipfw.edu>.

Willen, Matthew S. "Reflections on the Cultural Climate of Plagiarism." Liberal
    Education 90.4 (Fall2004 2004): 55–58. Academic Search Premier. EBSCO.
    Helmke Library, Fort Wayne, IN. 31 July 2008. <www.lib.ipfw.edu>.

ASSIGNMENT 9: EDITING A W233 STUDENT PAPER

The following student paper has numerous errors. Read the paper and circle all the errors you can find. Use proofreading marks where you know them.

Example W233 Essay

This essay was written as an argumentative paper for an ENG-W233 class. The student was asked to select a debatable issue, present both sides of the argument, and advocate one side. The criteria for the assignment were that the essay should:

- Contain an introduction paragraph that 1) introduces the audience to the issue being addressed, 2) identifies the writer's claim clearly, 3) examines why this information is important to the specified audience, and 4) announces the organization of the paper
- Offer solid evidence to support the writer's claim (statistics, facts, quotations, surveys)
- Represent and evaluate the opposing points of view fairly
- Argue reasonably against the opposition and for the writer's claim
- Maintain a clear focus toward the established audience throughout the paper
- Appeal to the identified audience in reason, as well as character and emotion
- Avoid fallacies or errors in reasoning
- Organize the material presented in a coherent, logical manner
- Contain a conclusion that 1) restates the writer's thesis, 2) summarizes the support for the writer's claim, and 3) echoes the introduction
- Use signals, cues, transitions, and paragraph hooks to achieve unity between ideas and paragraphs
- Use conventions of standard written English (appropriate diction, no omitted words, and grammar, punctuation, spelling)
- Include evidence of prewriting (freewrites, brainstorming sheets, research documents), drafts, criteria sheets, editing sheets, etc.
- Use seven (7) or more resources and accurately documented works cited, in addition to 10 or more resources on the bibliography page

B

B

Cover Letter

From: Tammy Student

To: Instructor Smith, ENG W233

Date: October 15, 2009

Subject: Vaccination Research Paper

Dear Readers:

Ok guys, this is my first draft. My purpose is to argue that vaccinations are good for kids. My audience is new parents and/or expecting parents...or really anyone who is interested in this issue. I'm very happy with my research right now, though I had a hard time finding information to support why parents shouldn't vaccinate their kids. I'm really happy with my visual—I think it adds to the paper nicely.

I'm concerned about my con section. I think it's too short. I also am not sure I cited right—in text or on my bib. I hope to get to the Writing Center to get some help on that one.

Any suggestions you can give me would help,

Tammy

Student 1

To Vaccinate or Not to Vaccinate: That Is the Question

As new parents prepare for the birth of a child, they are often inundated with information: how to care for their child, what supplies they'll need, the best ways to intellectually stimulate their baby, how to emotionally care for their baby. One of the first decisions that new parents make is regarding vaccinations. Some argue that you should vaccinate your baby following your doctor's advice; others argue that you should be more in control of your child's health. Unless you have a medical degree, however, making this important decision can become confusing and frustrating.

In the last few years, there has been a great debate about vaccinations between the medical community and parents. The resurgence of this debate started when "almost 10 years ago, a researcher in England created a major controversy when he and his colleagues published a report linking the measles-mumps-rubella (MMR) vaccine to the development of autism in children. ("Unexpected effect" par. 1). The desire of parents to prevent the development of autism in their children has caused many to begin to opt out of certain vaccination programs. Many in the medical community believe that this decision is irresponsible; however, it is ultimately the parents who must weigh the pros and cons of vaccinating their baby and make the decision themselves.

The Vaccination Schedule

The American Academy of Pediatrics offers parents and pediatricians guidelines for vaccinations. Figure 1 shows the schedule for 2009. In order for parents to make an informed decision about vaccinations, it's important

B

Student 2

to examine what each vaccination is. The decision to vaccinate or not vaccinate is not an all or nothing decision. Some parents may choose to adhere to part of the schedule or merely adjust their own timelines.

The Argument for Vaccination

The biggest argument for vaccination is that it can prevent your child from getting terrible diseases. Knopper writes:

> The current generation of parents making the decisions
> about vaccines doesn't remember polio and whooping cough
> outbreaks. The most vulnerable—newborns and the elderly—
> are not protected from these diseases. So an older kid could
> pass it on to a baby sister with disastrous results…."In a highly
> educated community like Boulder, or, say, the upper West Side
> of Manhattan, people feel that research is part of their job as
> parents. But they don't always know how to analyze medical
> reports, says Chana Goussetis, a Boulder health department
> communications specialist."

It makes more sense to have a discussion about parents' opinions about vaccinations with their doctor so they can make an informed decision.

Some argue that vaccinations are harmful to children and that the adverse reactions children get from vaccines do not make them worth the effort. However, in "Immunisation: are parents making informed decisions?" Marfe contends "Overwhelmingly, the majority of immunisations cause no harm but evidence reveals that there area very few that on rare occasions do so (Johnston 2003). For example, fewer than one child in a million develops encephalitis after MMR vaccine compared with between one in

200 and one in 5,000 who catches measles (NHS 2007)." These odds seem reasonable, but some parents do not want to play an odds game with their child's health. Physicians are concerned that fewer vaccinations or sporadic vaccinations may lead to the resurgence of illnesses thought to be eradicated in the United States. According to Currie, "A recent measles outbreak in the United States underscores the need to continue immunization programs and raise awareness about the ability of the disease to be imported from other countries.

Federal health officials who track measles cases declared the United States virtually free of the disease in 2000, with yearly reported cases between 2000 and 2007 ranging from 29 to 116. But in the first four months of 2008, 64 measles cases were reported in nine states and New York City. Fifty-four of the documented cases were imported from other countries, and 63 of the 64 measles patients had never been vaccinated against the disease." While this example addresses a patient who were imported, who's to say that in the future, we don't have a similar situation. If a child with rubella attends school in a classroom, half of which are vaccinated and half of which are not, is it possible there could be another rubella outbreak?

The Argument Against Vaccination

The phrase "the argument against vaccination" is a bit misleading. Most parents and physicians don't necessarily argue against all vaccination, but instead against either some vaccinations they may deem unnecessary or against the prescribed timetable of the APA. One of their biggest arguments is that children are given too many vaccinations today. According to Jenny McCarthy, "If you look at the vaccine schedule, and you can go on

B

B

www. generationrescue.com and that's a really good website…the vaccines that you received in 1983 were ten. Today they're thirty-six." Kimmet et al. report that almost 25 percent of parents believe that "children get more immunizations than are good for them."

Some parents argue that having a discussion about vaccinations with their doctors is very difficult. Levi reports, "Though pediatricians and family practice clinicians have a reputation as friendly and approachable, there are reports of parents having their concerns over immunization dismissed and/or disparaged, sometimes aggressively so. One recent study found that 24% to 39% of pediatricians reported they would dismiss a child from their practice if the parents refused 1 of the recommended vaccinations.50 It is not clear where these children would then go. But when parents' concerns are not effectively addressed, often the end result is that children do not get the medical care they need and deserve. " If a parent cannot have a reasonable discussion with his/her child's medical provider, then how can the parent be expected to make a reasonable decision?

Conclusion

It seems that it is easier to find research to support vaccinating your child than not. Perhaps this is because the medical community more readily disseminates scholarly material that their opponents. While it seems that following the APA's schedule for vaccinations is the way to go, ultimately, it's up to the parents to make decisions for their children.

Student 5

Bibliography

Abruzzese, Sarah. "Maryland Parents Told to Have Children Immunized." New York Times (18 Nov. 2007): 36. Academic Search Premier. EBSCO. Helmke Library, Fort Wayne, IN. 31 July 2008. <www.lib.ipfw.edu>.

Baker, Jeffrey P. "Mercury, Vaccines, and Autism One Controversy, Three Histories." American Journal of Public Health 98.2 (Feb. 2008): 244–253. Academic Search Premier. EBSCO. Helmke Library, Fort Wayne, IN. 31 July 2008. <www.lib.ipfw.edu>.

Currie, Donya. "Measles outbreak in two states reported." Nation's Health 38.5 (June 2008): 8–8. Academic Search Premier. EBSCO. Helmke Library, Fort Wayne, IN. 31 July 2008. <www.lib.ipfw.edu>.

Diggle, Linda. "Schedule timing and booster vaccinations." Practice Nurse 34.4 (07 Sep. 2007): 9–9. Academic Search Premier. Helmke Library, Fort Wayne, IN. 31 July 2008. <www.lib.ipfw.edu>.

K. L. "Immunization Facts." Working Mother 30.8 (Nov. 2007): 98-98. Academic Search Premier. EBSCO. Helmke Library, Fort Wayne, IN. 31 July 2008 . <www.lib.ipfw.edu>.

Kimmel, Sanford R., et al. "Addressing immunization barriers, benefits, and risks." Journal of Family Practice 56.2 (02 Feb. 2007): S61–S69. Academic Search Premier. EBSCO. Helmke Library, Fort Wayne, IN.31 July 2008. <www.lib. ipfw.edu>.

Knopper, Melissa. "Calling the Shots." E—The Environmental Magazine 18.4 (July 2007): 40–41. Academic Search Premier. EBSCO. Helmke Library, Fort Wayne, IN. 31 July 2008. <www.lib.ipfw.edu>.

Kotz, Deborah. "Fewer Sticks at Vaccination Time." U.S. News & World Report 142.7 (26 Feb. 2007): 66–66. Academic Search Premier. EBSCO. Helmke Library, Fort Wayne, IN. 31 July 2008. <www.lib.ipfw.edu>.

Lett, Dan. "Vaccine—autism link discounted, but effect of "study" is unknown." CMAJ: Canadian Medical Association Journal 177.8 (09 Oct. 2007): 841–841. Academic Search Premier. EBSCO. Helmke Library, Fort Wayne, IN. 31 July 2008. <www.lib.ipfw.edu>.

Levi, Benjamin H. "Addressing Parents' Concerns About Childhood Immunizations: A Tutorial for Primary Care Providers." Pediatrics 120.1 (July 2007): 18–26. Academic Search Premier. EBSCO. Helmke Library, Fort Wayne, IN. 31 July 2008. <www.lib.ipfw.edu>.

B

B

Student 6

Marfé, Eileen. "Immunisation: are parents making informed decisions?." Paediatric Nursing 19.5 (June 2007): 20–22. Academic Search Premier. EBSCO. Helmke Library, Fort Wayne, IN. 31 July 2008. <www.lib.ipfw.edu>.

"No link found between MMR jab and autism." Practice Nurse 35.4 (22 Feb. 2008): 8–8. Academic Search Premier. EBSCO. Helmke Library, Fort Wayne, IN. 31 July 2008. <www.lib.ipfw.edu>.

Moore, Alison. "Another injection?." Nursing Standard 22.18 (09 Jan. 2008): 23–23. Academic Search Premier. EBSCO. Helmke Library, Fort Wayne, IN. 31 July 2008. <www.lib.ipfw.edu>.

"On message, off target." Nature 452.7184 (13 Mar. 2008): 128–128. Academic Search Premier. EBSCO. Helmke Library, Fort Wayne, IN. 31 July 2008. <www.lib.ipfw.edu>.

"Preventing illness through immunization." American Nurse 39.3 (May 2007): 5–5. Academic Search Premier. EBSCO. Helmke Library, Fort Wayne, IN. 31 July 2008. <www.lib.ipfw.edu>.

"Recommended Immunization Schedules for Persons Aged 0-18 Years—United States, 2008." MMWR: Morbidity & Mortality Weekly Report 57.1 (11 Jan. 2008): Q-1–Q-4. Academic Search Premier. EBSCO. Helmke Library, Fort Wayne, IN. 31 July 2008. <www.lib.ipfw.edu>.

"Reducing The Pain During Children's Immunizations. (Cover story)." Child Health Alert 25 (June 2007): 1–1. Academic Search Premier. EBSCO. Helmke Library, Fort Wayne, IN. 31 July 2008. <www.lib.ipfw.edu>.

Shimabukuro, Tom T., et al. "Potential for Improving Age- Appropriate Vaccination Coverage by Maximizing the 18-Month Well-Child Visit." Journal of Public Health Management & Practice 13.6 (Nov. 2007): 572–577. Academic Search Premier. EBSCO. Helmke Library, Fort Wayne, IN. 31 July 2008. <www.lib.ipfw.edu>.

Spencer, Jane. "States Relax Child Vaccine Laws." Wall Street Journal—Eastern Edition 240.27 (07 Aug. 2002): D1. Academic Search Premier. EBSCO. Helmke Library, Fort Wayne, IN. 31 July 2008. <www.lib.ipfw.edu>.

Steinhauer, Jennifer, and Gardiner Harris.. "Rising Public Health Risk Seen As More Parents Reject Vaccines." New York Student 9 Times (21 Mar. 2008): 1. Academic Search Premier. EBSCO. Helmke Library, Fort Wayne, IN. 31 July 2008. <www.lib.ipfw.edu>.

Student 7

Temte, Jonathan L., and Doug Campos-Outcalt.. "ACIP Releases 2008 Child and Adolescent Immunization Schedules." American Family Physician 77.1 (Jan. 2008): 96–97. Academic Search Premier. EBSCO. Helmke Library, Fort Wayne, IN. 31 July 2008. <www.lib.ipfw.edu>.

"An Unexpected Effect Of The Autism-Vaccine Controversy." Child Health Alert 25 (May 2007): 3–4. Academic Search Premier. EBSCO. Helmke Library, Fort Wayne, IN. 31 July 2008. <www.lib.ipfw.edu>.

"Updated Pediatric Immunization Guidelines." Nurse Practitioner 33.7 (July 2008): 49–49. Academic Search Premier. EBSCO. Helmke Library, Fort Wayne, IN. 31 July 2008. <www.lib.ipfw.edu>.

"Vaccinations: One More Has Been Added…." Child Health Alert 25 (Apr. 2007): 5-5. Academic Search Premier. EBSCO. Helmke Library, Fort Wayne, IN. 31 July 2008 . <www.lib.ipfw.edu>.

Webb, Jeremy. "Editorial: Clarity needed over autism and vaccines." New Scientist 197.2646 (08 Mar. 2008): 5-5. Academic Search Premier. EBSCO. Helmke Library, Fort Wayne, IN. 31 July 2008. <www.lib.ipfw.edu>.

B

B